TEACHABLES

FROM

TRASHABLES

HOMEMADE TOYS
THAT TEACH

BY REDLEAF PRESS
TEXT & DRAWINGS by C. EMMA LINDERMAN

Published by: Redleaf Press
                  Formerly Toys 'n Things Press
                  a division of Resources for Child Caring
                  450 North Syndicate, Suite 5
                  St. Paul, Minnesota 55104

Distributed by: Gryphon House
                  PO Box 275
                  Mt. Rainier, Maryland 20712

Library of Congress Catalog Card No. 79 - 64910

ISBN: 0-934140-00-6

Printed in the United States of America.

THE PEOPLE WHO HELPED CREATE THIS BOOK

For the past six years many people who care about children in Ramsey County Minnesota have helped to develop a "homemade toys that teach" philosophy within their caregiving community. As members and staff of Toys 'n Things they contributed the idea seeds and the enthusiastic support needed for Teachables from Trashables to blossom into this publishable treasure. A special thank you must go to Lucille Burnham, Greg Fortney, Bettye Willis, Ardis Kysar, Rhoda Redleaf and Audrey Robertson whose investment of time and talents in creative toymaking are freely reflected. Appreciation is also expressed to Bruce Ecker and Kathy Lugosch for their warm support and imaginative suggestions during the writing of this book.

CONTENTS

WHAT THIS BOOK IS ALL ABOUT.................................... 7

HOW THIS BOOK IS ORGANIZED.................................... 8

GOOD TOYS CAN MEET THE KID-PROOF TEST...................... 9

BEFORE YOU BEGIN.. 10

ALUMINUM PIE TIN TOY:
    Hanging Mobiles.. 11

CARDBOARD BOX TOYS:
    Cause & Effect Match Board............................. 14
    Crawl-Over Box.. 17
    Dancing Limber Jenny or Joe........................... 19
    Felt Board.. 23
    Reversible Color & Design Sign........................ 26

CARDBOARD CONE TOYS:
    Binoculars.. 29
    Pop-Up Puppet... 31

CARDBOARD TUBE TOYS:
    Baker's Hat and Rolling Pin............................ 36
    Colored Button Sort.................................... 39
    Kazoo... 42
    Musical Roller Pull Toy............................... 44
    Ring Catch.. 46

CLOTH OR CARPET TOYS:
    Carpet Puzzles... 48
    Easy Grasp Ball.. 50
    Fabric Matching Game.................................. 54
    Feel & Tell Box.. 56
    Following Footsteps Game.............................. 58
    Milking Cow.. 60
    Stuffed Kick Toy....................................... 64
    Texture Ball... 67

CLOTHES PIN TOY:
    Clothespin Matching Game.............................. 70

COCOA CAN TOY:
    Box Camera... 72

EGG CARTON TOY:
    Styrofoam Bubble Boat................................. 74

ENVELOPE TOY:
    Mail Sorting Game..................................... 76

FOAM RUBBER TOY:

    Foam Block Push Through.. 78

GLOVE TOY:

    Finger Puppets.. 81

LID TOYS:

    Lid Matching Puzzles... 83
    Lid Puppets.. 85
    Plastic Lacing Cards... 88
    Rhythm Shakers... 90
    Wagon.. 92

MAGAZINE TOY:

    Picture Puzzle... 95

MILK CARTON TOY:

    Milk Carton Blocks... 99

NEWSPAPER TOY:

    Sliding Egg...102

PAPER BAG TOYS:

    Back Pack & Sit-Upon..105
    Mail Carrier's Cap and Bag.....................................108

PLASTIC CONTAINER TOYS:

    Bug Keeper...111
    Face Masks...113
    Fish Bowl Shaker Bottle..117
    Painter's Visor, Pail & Roller.................................120
    Scoop Catch..124

PLASTIC SANDWICH BAG TOY:

    Sandwich Bag Picture Book......................................126

SOCK TOY:

    Riding Horse...129

TAGBOARD TOYS:

    Board Game...132
    Dominoes...136
    Matching Puzzles...139
    Picture Matching Game..143

THREAD SPOOL TOY:

    Spool Snake..145

TIN CAN TOYS:

Bongo Drum.....................................147
Nesting Cans...................................150
Pom Pom Grasp & Pull Toy.......................152
Self Help Sally (or Sam).......................156
Shape Sorting Can..............................161
Tin Can Musical Rolling Pin....................163
Tin Can Stilts.................................166

WIRE HANGER TOYS:

Butterfly Net..................................168
Crib Mobile....................................170
Paddle Ball....................................173
Pulley Toy.....................................175

TOYS GROUPED ACCORDING TO AGE GROUP GUIDELINES.............178

THERE'S MORE TO COME.................................181

WHAT THIS BOOK IS ALL ABOUT

This book has been written as a beginning, as a catalyst for new and not-yet-thought-of ways to turn household "junk" objects into inexpensive, safe and educational toys for children.   The toys and instructions here are regarded as modifiable examples that will hopefully help you generate new ideas.

The needs and interests of particular children, as well as the materials you have available, should be kept in mind as you read this book. You are encouraged to substitute different materials for those suggested here, to write notes to yourself about what did or did not work, and to record new toy ideas that have been successful for you.

You may wish to begin a "toy junk" box for clean household objects you would normally throw away. (Stores, factories, and local recycling distribution centers are also good places to find "junked" materials.) Then, when you are ready to make some toys, you will have a treasure chest of materials awaiting you.

Take a little time to stretch your imagination and explore the possible uses of these materials. As you begin, experiment with how the object feels and sounds. What happens if you drop it, tap it, roll it or squeese it? Try tearing or cutting it up and then see how it changes. What new uses might it now have? The possibilities are endless. Practice using your imagination and curiousity and you may be amazed at the results. Encourage your children to help in this process, as well as in the toy-making, for they may prove to be great innovators themselves.

When choosing a toy to make, it is also important to think about how the toy might be used by your child and what it teaches - what skills the child can learn and/or practice by playing with the toy. To help you think about toys in this way, we have included starter suggestions about how to use each toy and what it does in terms of the child's learning. More about this is explained on the next page, so please keep reading.

HOW THIS BOOK IS ORGANIZED

The toy making ideas are presented alphabetically in categories based on the main materials needed to make each toy such as tin cans, cardboard tubes, etc.

The age groups for which each toy is most appropriate are listed below the toy's title. The four age group categories we chose to use - infants, toddlers, preschool and school age - are considered general guidelines and are based on the kinds of skills and interests a child typically develops at these ages. The age groups given here should not be viewed as absolutes. Each child grows and develops at his or her own pace. She or he may therefore be "ready" to enjoy and learn from these toys at times that differ from our guidelines. Also, keep in mind that the same toy may be used by children of different ages in different ways since a good toy is often a versatile toy. There were usually many more uses for the toys than could be described. Consider both the age group guidelines, and your understanding of the child's skills and interests, when choosing which toys to make.

The age group guidelines are related to the "How To Use It" and "What It Does" boxes. The "How To Use It" box suggests activities in which the toy could be used. Again, these suggestions should not be used to limit the creativity of the child but are, instead, some beginning ideas. The "What It Does" box explains what skills these activities help to teach and develop in a child. It may seem surprising to think of toys in terms of what they "teach", but the play of children makes up a very large part of their growing experience with the world. Children are constantly learning and practicing new skills as they interact with toys, from an infant beginning to focus on the brightly colored objects of a hanging mobile, to the problem-solving of an older child putting together the pieces of a carpet puzzle. All are part of the growth process.

The many skills that make up the growth process have been grouped by some toy libraries and child development training programs into five broad areas or processes. These processes are listed in the "What It Does" box as they apply to the activities for each toy. Each process includes skills that generally serve a similar developmental purpose:

Physical Development Process skills are learned through the body, including large and small muscle movement.

Sensory & Perceptual Process skills use the five senses, sometimes alone or in different combinations.

Social & Emotional Process skills deal with feelings, getting along with other people, understanding oneself and one's community, and being able to help oneself.

Cognitive & Symbolic Process skills are learned through the mind: "thinking" skills like speaking, reading, understanding basic concepts, science, etc.

Creative Process skills deal with "spirit": imagination, problem solving, drama, etc.

These five processes are often happening all at once or in different combinations, and a well-rounded toy collection will include some toys that tap each of these processes. It is hoped that this way of organizing the many skills of growing will help you to choose toys that will encourage optimal growth and healthy development for your children!

GOOD TOYS CAN MEET THE "KID-PROOFED" TESTS

The safety needs of children should always be kept in mind as toys are made. "Kid-proofed toys must meet these tests:

1. **THEY ARE CLEAN.**

   Wash all materials and containers thoroughly before using.

2. **THEY HAVE NO SHARP EDGES.**

   Corners should be rounded or taped; materials that might splinter should be sanded and oiled.

3. **THEY ARE TOO BIG TO BE SWALLOWED.**

   A general rule is that any object should be about 1" x 1/2" in size. If you must use small objects, tie a few of them together to make them bigger.

4. **THEY ARE MADE OF NONTOXIC MATERIALS.**

   Do not use any material that could be harmful if eaten, chewed or smelled! Read package instructions to make sure that markers and glue or other adhesives are nontoxic and safe for use with children.

NOTE: Although the instructions for toys in this book have been written with the "kid-proofed" tests in mind, no one can guarantee the absolute safety of these toys or procedures. We urge parents and teachers to use care and common sense to make all toys as safe as possible.

BEFORE YOU BEGIN

Once you have chosen a toy, it is suggested that you read through the "What You Need To Make It" and "How To Make It" instructions before beginning. Then, you can decide best whether you want to substitute some materials for those given.

Every effort has been made to use tools and materials in this book that are generally available to everyone. Here are a few suggestions about some of the materials as they apply to toymaking:

<u>Glue</u>: All purpose white glues are usually marked "nontoxic" and, if so, are good for toymaking. Many other glues contain substances that could be harmful if swallowed, so be sure to check the glue you use. If the bottle is not marked "nontoxic", choose another brand that is!

<u>Felt tip markers</u>: These add color and are easy to use, but they do have limitations. "Permanent" markers are usually toxic and should be avoided. Waterbased markers are usually safe, but toys made with them should be covered with clear contact paper if there is any chance they might be chewed on or become wet. Cutting out shapes in contact paper instead of using a marker is often just as good.

<u>Contact paper</u>: Used often in this book, it allows toys once made to be cleaned easily and may increase the life of the toy. Brightly colored contact paper also helps attract a child's attention to the toy. Usually found in variety stores, it is felt that contact paper is a good investment for any serious toy maker.

<u>Tools</u>: Some of the household tools mentioned in this book are sharp or heavy, and are best used only by an adult. If your children help in the making of the toys, please be careful about this possible hazard.

Now, as you turn this page, remember that this book is a resource and a beginning:

USE YOUR IMAGINATION!

HANGING MOBILES

AGE GROUP: INFANT

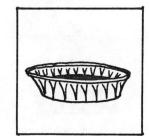

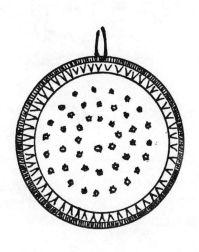

HOW TO USE IT:

Hang the mobile securely to a window rod or ceiling fixture within the sight of the infant. <u>The objects should be out of reach of the child!</u> The mobile will move in the breeze. Objects can be changed from time to time — see the "New Objects" note for "Crib Mobile" in Part I.

<u>Safety Note</u>: If you have curious toddlers or other small children who may try to "investigate" the mobile, it is wise to hang it away from windows.

WHAT IT DOES:

Bright colors and movement attract the baby's attention to the objects, and encourage focusing, eye movements, and general visual development.

(Sensory & Perceptual Process)

WHAT YOU NEED TO MAKE IT:

aluminum pie tin

assorted colorful household objects

juice can with 1 end removed

YARN

scissors

nail

OR string, fishing line, wire, etc.

button

HOW TO MAKE IT:

① Punch small holes in the pie tin with a hammer and nail to make a design. (Place the area to be punched over the open end of the empty can.)

② If the edges of the holes are sharp, they can be flattened with the unopened end of the juice can.
   Hang the tin with yarn.

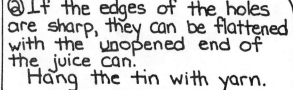

flatten hole edges with this

YARN

OR: ① Punch holes as described above along the rim of the pie tin. Also punch one hole in the middle. Thread yarn through the holes.

② Hang objects from the yarn attached to the rim. Tie a fat knot at the other end. Balance them!
Tie a knot around a button on the bottom side of the middle piece of yarn. Make a loop at the other end, and hang the mobile by this loop.

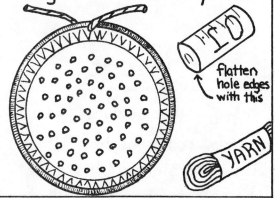

MOBILE VARIATIONS ARE ENDLESS!

Any item can be hung by itself or in whatever balanced combination you make.

Bold, bright colors will attract the baby best. ("Baby" blue and pink are not bright enough!)

Make the mobiles interesting from a crib vantage point... see what they look like from the baby's viewpoint.

Important! Make sure objects are secure and won't fall off-give them a good shake to be certain.

Hang mobiles by: string
yarn
fishing line
telephone cord
old slinky sections
etc.

Hang them on: curtain rods
clothes hangers
wooden dowels
tree branches
heavy cardboard "donuts"
etc.

Hang: feathers
plastic fruit
wooden utensils
yarn fuzz balls
cardboard shapes
thread spools
shiny objects
drinking straw sculptures
plastic eating utensils
seed packets
pictures mounted on cardboard
tinker toy sculptures
pieces of plastic bottles
egg carton pieces
ANYTHING BOLD, BRIGHT and LIGHT!

CAUSE & EFFECT MATCH BOARD

AGE GROUP: INFANT, (EARLY) TODDLER

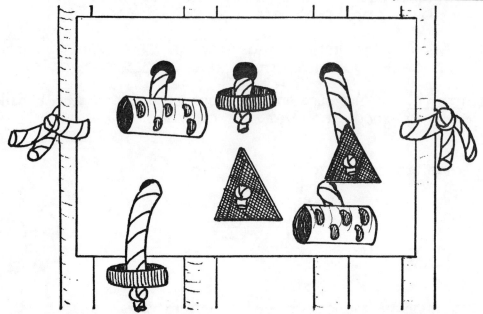

HOW TO USE IT:

The board is tied securely to the side of the crib. Similar objects are attached to the back of the board with string, so that when one object is pulled by the child, its match also moves in the opposite direction!

When you first introduce this toy, let the baby explore the objects attached to it. Demonstrate a few times how the objects can be pulled. Then let the baby experiment on his or her own.

Share in the delight of the movement with your child!

WHAT IT DOES:

Bright colors attract the baby to the toy and encourage eye focusing. The cause and effect action of this toy appeals to the infant's interest in movement and change, and encourages the baby to actively take part in making change happen.

It also encourages an awareness of sameness, shapes, and colors, while encouraging the development of grasping and pulling skills.

(Sensory & Perceptual, Cognitive & Symbolic, Physical Development Processes)

WHAT YOU NEED TO MAKE IT:

8" x 11" heavy cardboard

3"x4" cardboard

sturdy string OR cord

matte knife

contact paper (2 contrasting colors)

2 pairs of matching items: like plastic lids and plastic curlers

large nail

pliers OR potholder

stove top

HOW TO MAKE IT:

①Cover each piece of cardboard with a different color of contact paper.

②Cut a hole in 2 opposite sides of the large cardboard piece. Thread a 12" piece of string through each hole.

③Cut 6 holes in the large cardboard piece.

④Make a hole in the middle of each jar lid with a hot nail (by heating the nail on the stove).

⑤ Cut the small cardboard piece into 2 triangles and make a hole in the middle of each one.

cut

⑥ Cut 3 pieces of string: 20", 16" and 16." Tie a knot in one end of each one. Put one of each object on a string as shown.

⑦ Beginning on the contact paper side of the board, lace each string through 2 holes. (Lace the longest string through holes at opposite ends of the board.)

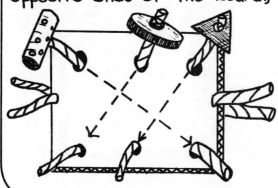

⑧ Thread the matching object on each string and tie a knot.

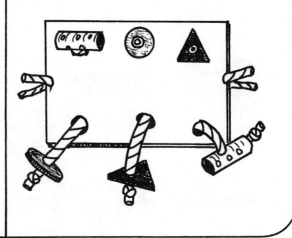

BOARD MAKING HINTS

Colors should be bold and bright, and each pair of matching objects should be a different color from the other pairs of objects.

Matching item ideas: yarn pom poms
wooden spools
rubber balls
soap bottle ends
etc.

Make sure everything is fastened <u>securely</u>!

CRAWL-OVER BOX

AGE GROUP: (CRAWLING) INFANT

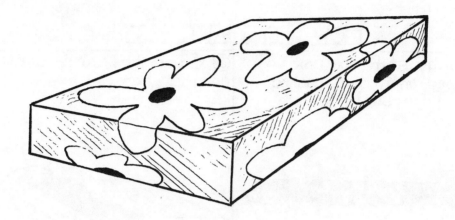

HOW TO USE IT:

Place the box on the floor. Crawling infants enjoy crawling over it or pushing it along the floor.

WHAT IT DOES:

The box provides a safe object for experimenting with, and practicing, a variation of crawling: crawling <u>over</u>. The crawl-over box encourages the development of leg and arm muscles, and improves large muscle coordination.

(Physical Development Process)

WHAT YOU NEED TO MAKE IT:

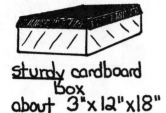
sturdy cardboard box
about 3"x 12"x 18"

old newspapers

colorful contact paper

tape

HOW TO MAKE IT:

① Tightly stuff the box with newspaper until it is packed firm. Tape shut.

② Cover the entire box with contact paper.

OTHER IDEAS

✳ Rope handles may be added to two sides.

✳ Stuff milk carton blocks and tape them together before covering with contact paper to make crawl-over boxes of different shapes.

✳ Little "stairs" for advanced crawlers and toddlers can be made by taping 2 shallow boxes of different sizes together. Be sure they are sturdy, well stuffed, and placed so there is no "drop-off". (Tape together before covering with contact paper.)

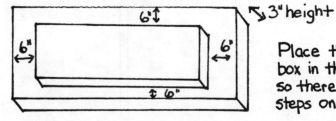

6"

6"

6"

6"

3" height

(bird's eye view)

Place the second box in the middle so there are 2 steps on every side.

Dancing LimberJenny or Joe

Age Group: Preschool, SchoolAge

How To Use It:

The child sits on one end of the wooden paddle. (It works best if this is done on a hard chair or bench.) Holding the LimberJenny so her feet are just above the other end of the paddle, the child then taps the middle of the paddle. This makes the LimberJenny dance! (Jiggling the pencil a bit also helps.) The LimberJenny is a fun rhythm instrument; she dances to music or all by herself. Without the paddle she becomes a puppet!

What It Does:

The LimberJenny helps to make music a "seeing and doing" as well as a listening activity, and by so doing it encourages an awareness of, and interest in, rhythms and music. The LimberJenny encourages creative musical and dramatic expression, and also helps to develop hand coordination.

(Creative, Physical Development Processes)

WHAT YOU NEED TO MAKE IT:

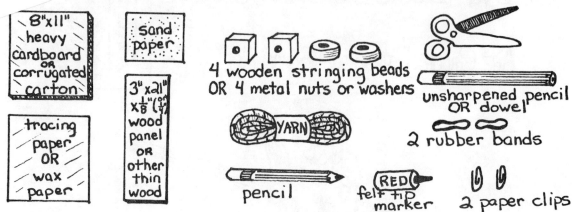

8"x11" heavy cardboard OR corrugated carton

tracing paper OR wax paper

sand paper

3"x21" x 1/8" (3") wood panel OR other thin wood

4 wooden stringing beads OR 4 metal nuts or washers

YARN

pencil

scissors

unsharpened pencil OR dowel

2 rubber bands

RED felt tip marker

2 paper clips

HOW TO MAKE IT:

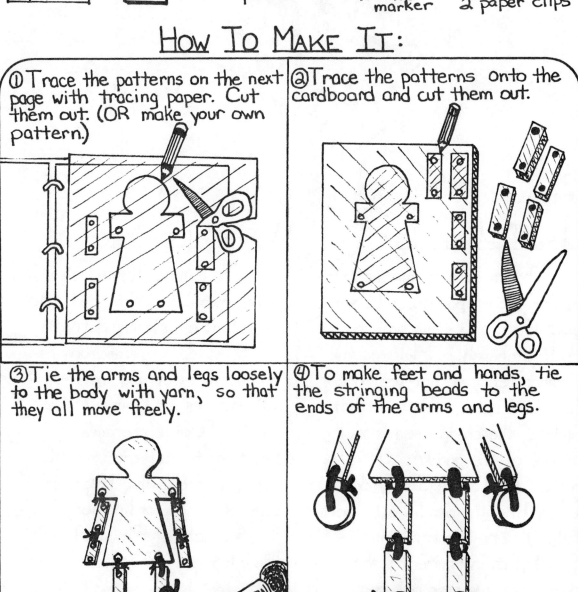

① Trace the patterns on the next page with tracing paper. Cut them out. (OR make your own pattern.)

② Trace the patterns onto the cardboard and cut them out.

③ Tie the arms and legs loosely to the body with yarn, so that they all move freely.

④ To make feet and hands, tie the stringing beads to the ends of the arms and legs.

TRACE THESE PATTERNS

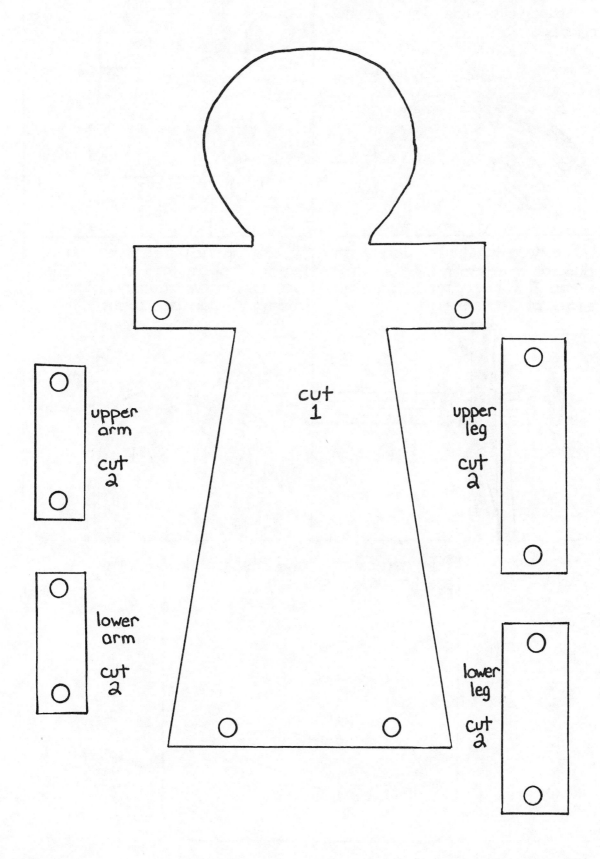

upper
arm

cut
2

lower
arm

cut
2

cut
1

upper
leg

cut
2

lower
leg

cut
2

⑤ Make a small hole near the top of the head and tie yarn through it as shown. Paper clip earrings can be made by poking the paper clip ends through the cardboard.

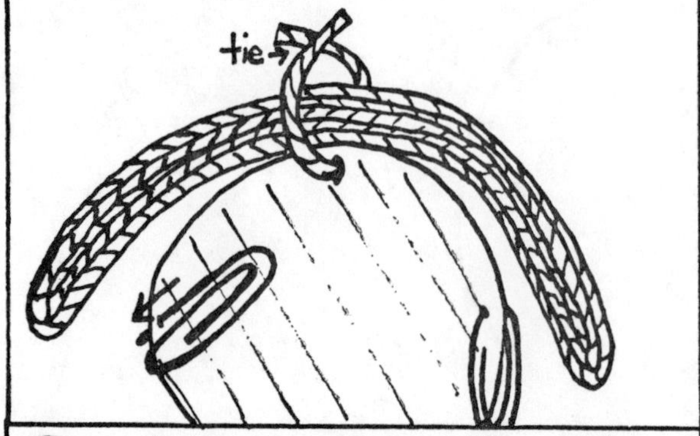

tie →

⑥ In the upper torso, make a hole just big enough for a pencil to fit snugly through it.

⑦ To keep the limber Jenny from dancing right off the pencil, wrap 2 rubber bands on either side of the pencil.

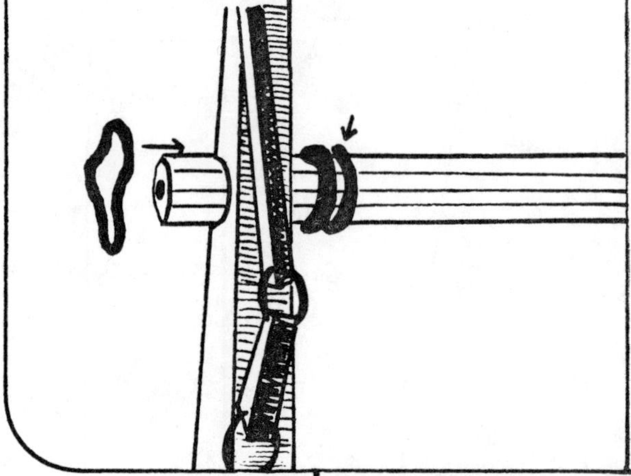

⑧ Draw facial features on both sides of the face. (This way both the child and the audience can see a face.)

RED

draw on the other side too!

⑨ If necessary, sand the wooden paddle until smooth.

FELT BOARD

AGE GROUP: PRESCHOOL, SCHOOL AGE

HOW TO USE IT:

Pieces of colored felt, cut into many shapes, will stick to the felt board, and can be arranged to make designs. (Letters & numbers can be added for school-agers.) It can be used as an open-ended art activity, to illustrate stories, or as a matching game (matching the designs of another person or copying designs drawn on cards). Tic-tac-toe, counting, or shape & color naming games can be played. Feelings expression and body awareness activities are also possible with felt body parts such as smiles, frowns, heads, eyes, etc.

WHAT IT DOES:

It encourages art expression and allows the child to experiment freely (especially since the designs can be so easily changed). It encourages a familiarity with shapes, colors, numbers & letters, and helps to develop matching and naming skills (that will help with later reading and math understanding). It can help body awareness and self concept, and also social skills.

(Creative, Cognitive & Symbolic, Social & Emotional Processes)

What You Need To Make It:

 sturdy cardboard box

OR piece of wood, tagboard, linoleum tile, etc.

glue

matte knife

 pieces of colored felt : 1 piece must be as large as one side of the box. NOTE: <u>polyester</u> felt does <u>NOT</u> work.
OR colored tagboard backed with corduroy or flannel; the nappy side of the material will stick to the nappy material on the board.

 tin can & lid
OR box & lid, plastic bag, etc. <u>DO</u> <u>NOT</u> use a plastic bag if this toy will be used around infants, toddlers or preschoolers!

How To Make It:

① Cut the box with the matte knife as shown. Use this part for the feltboard.

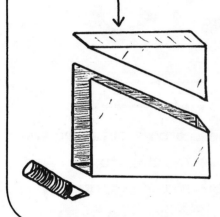

② Cut a piece of felt to cover the largest rectangular side of the feltboard. Glue the felt to this side of the board.

③ Cut out felt shapes, letters or numbers, etc. of different colors and sizes. Store them in the can.

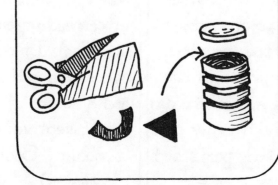

OTHER FELT BOARD IDEAS...
...CAN YOU THINK OF MORE?

Designs to copy may be drawn on construction paper, index cards, or old playing cards. (Glue paper over the pictures on the playing cards.) Holes can be punched with a paper punch and yarn tied through the holes for easy keeping.

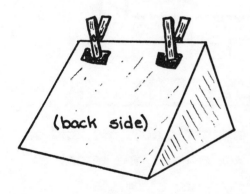

(back side)

The board can be a painting or drawing easel, too! Cut as in step ①. Cut 2 holes in the back side near the top - as shown. Paper can be secured to the front with clothespins! Egg cartons make great paint containers.

For school agers: felt boards can be taken on car trips. Store felt pieces in a plastic bag for easy finding.

Reversible Color & Design Sign

Age Group: Infant

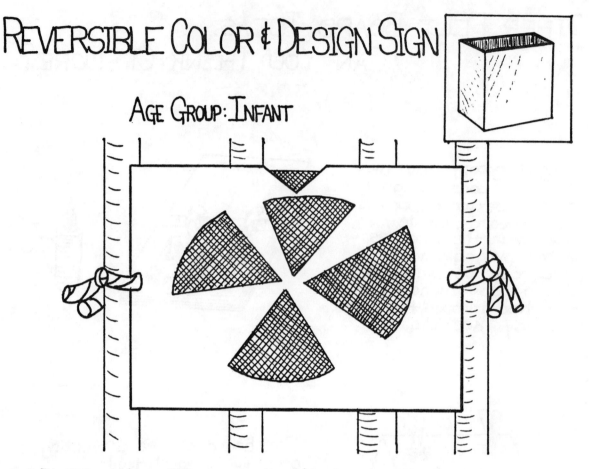

How To Use It:

Hang the sign securely within the infant's sight, on a wall or a window sill, or hang it as a mobile. The designs and colored cards facing the baby can be changed every few days. (Change the color one day, the designs another.)

The designs can be all kinds of things—abstract bold patterns, musical notes, butterflies, faces, etc. Use your imagination!

What It Does:

Bright colors and bold designs attract the infant to the sign and encourage focusing, awareness of colors and shapes, and help general visual development.

Changing the colors and designs (as well as the movement when used as a mobile) gives the baby a variety of visual experiences.

(Sensory & Perceptual Process)

WHAT YOU NEED TO MAKE IT:

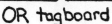
2 pieces of cardboard each about 9"x12"

OR tagboard

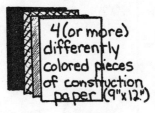
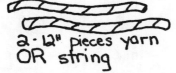
4 (or more) differently colored pieces of construction paper (9"x12")

clear contact paper

glue

pencil

2 · 12" pieces yarn
OR string

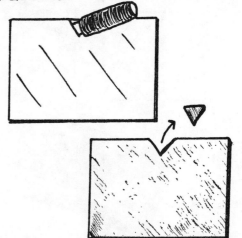
matte knife
OR sharp scissors

HOW TO MAKE IT:

① Glue one piece of construction paper to each piece of cardboard. Cover with contact paper.

contact paper

glue

construction paper

cardboard

② Cut a notch in the middle of one side of each piece of cardboard.

③ Leaving a one inch margin on each side, draw a bold design in the middle of each cardboard. (It is best if SIMPLE and LARGE.) Make each design different.

1" margin

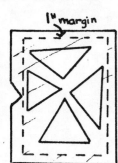

④ Cut out the designs.

⑤Glue the 2 cardboard pieces together, <u>colored side out</u>, along the <u>3 unnotched edges only</u>.

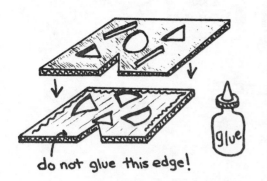

do not glue this edge!

⑥Make a hole in the 2 unnotched opposite sides of the cardboard. Lace a piece of yarn through each hole. (Make only one hole for a mobile)

⑦Cut off 1 inch on 3 sides of the remaining pieces of construction paper.

1"

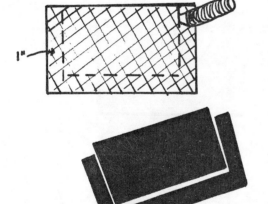

⑧Slip these 2 pieces of construction paper between the cardboard pieces at the notched edge (so a different color shows through for each design).

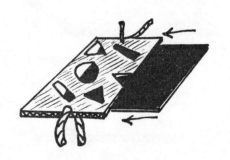

⑧Tie the board to the crib within sight of the baby. Both the designs and the colors can be easily switched around.

BINOCULARS

AGE GROUP: PRESCHOOL, SCHOOL AGE

HOW TO USE IT:

Binoculars are worn around the neck and are used in dramatic play to imitate real binoculars by looking through one end. Safari, opera, or ballpark adventures are a few suggestions for make-believe use of the binoculars.

WHAT IT DOES:

Binoculars encourage creative dramatics. They also help children become more aware of how they use their eyes in many activities.

(Creative, Sensory & Perceptual Processes)

What You Need To Make It:

2 cardboard thread or string cones
OR 2 sturdy tubes

2 to 3 ft string

strong tape

2 thick rubber bands

cellophane OR plastic wrap

glue

How To Make It:

① Cover the widest end of each tube with cellophane and secure with a rubber band.

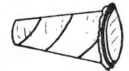

② Glue the edges of the cellophane and the rubber band (to make sure they do not come off).

glue here too

③ Tie a knot in each end of the string.

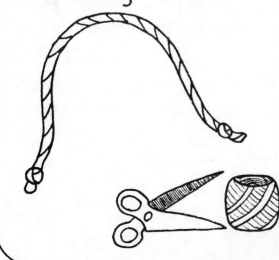

④ With one end of the string on either side, hold the 2 cones together and wind tape around them.

POP-UP PUPPET

AGE GROUP: INFANT, TODDLER, PRESCHOOL, SCHOOL AGE

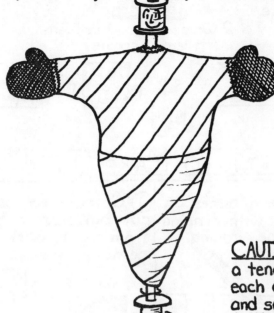

CAUTION: children have a tendency to poke each other with this toy and so it requires some initial supervision.

HOW TO USE IT:

Young children delight in appearing-disappearing toys (like the traditional jack-in-the-box): when the dowel is pulled away from the cone, the puppet disappears into the cone. When it is pushed up, the puppet pops up! With infants and young toddlers, adults can play peek-a-boo games with the puppets; older children enjoy making this happen themselves.

Puppets can be used to act out stories, make up plays, express feelings, and other creative activities, alone or with others.

WHAT IT DOES:

Learning that objects and people are permanent—that they still exist even when out of sight of the child—is a process that young children explore as they grow. The puppet helps children understand and actively make this appearance and disappearance happen. It also helps to develop an understanding of cause and effect. Puppets encourage creative dramatics, talking and expressing feelings, and listening and sharing skills.

(Social & Emotional, Creative, Cognitive & Symbolic Processes)

WHAT YOU NEED TO MAKE IT:

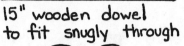

2½" diameter cardboard thread cone OR sturdy tube

15" wooden dowel to fit snugly through

½ yard colorful cloth

2 wooden or styrofoam thread spools

tracing paper OR wax paper

glue

2"x2" polyester felt

2"x2" Contact paper

baby oil

sand paper

OR mineral oil

HOW TO MAKE IT:

① Trace the pattern pieces on the next 2 pages with tracing paper. Cut out the tracing paper patterns.

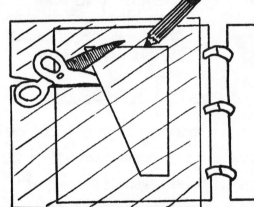

② Using the patterns just cut out, cut out puppet hands from felt, and the other pattern pieces from cloth.

felt

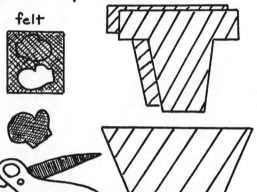

③ Folding in at the dotted lines, sew the "puppet body" pieces together, stitching as shown. Gather the wrist a bit and sew on the hands.

leave open

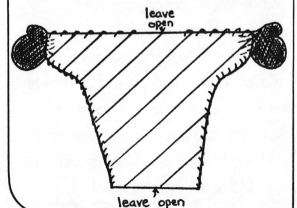

leave open

④ Glue the bottom of the puppet body around the wide end of the cone. Folding under at the dotted lines as shown on the pattern, glue the "cone material" piece around the cone.

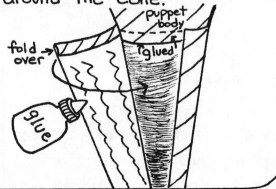

puppet body

fold over

glued

glue

Trace these patterns with tracing paper. These patterns fit a cone with a 2½" diameter (and about a 6½" height). Modify the pattern accordingly if your cone or tube is a different size.

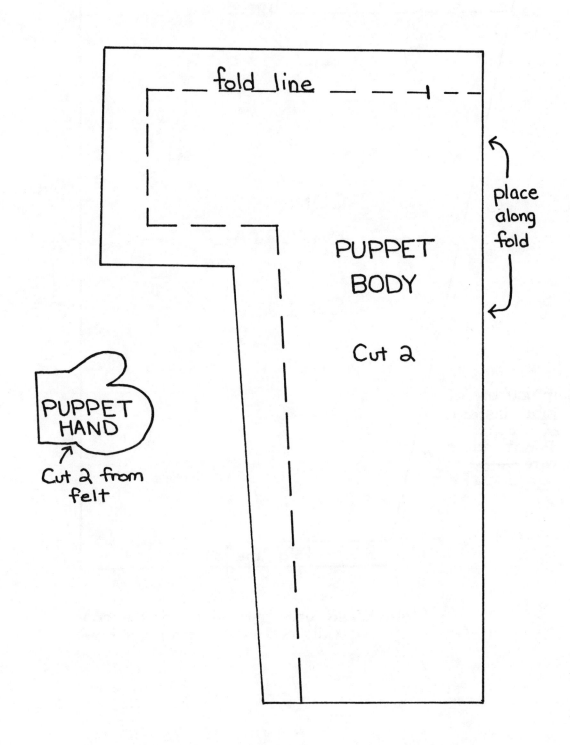

fold line

PUPPET BODY

Cut 2

place along fold

PUPPET HAND

Cut 2 from felt

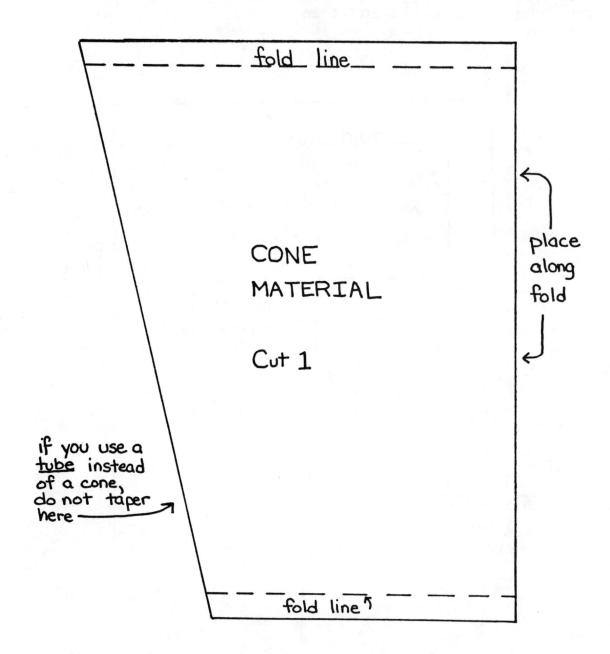

fold line

CONE

MATERIAL

Cut 1

place along fold

if you use a tube instead of a cone, do not taper here

fold line

Note: When you glue this to the cone it will probably overlap some.

⑤Sand the dowel until smooth. Rub it with baby oil.

⑥Insert the dowel through the cone and the puppet neck. Gather and/or glue the neck opening around the dowel.

⑦Glue a spool to each end of the dowel.

⑧Make a face on the puppet head with contact paper.

Baker's Hat & Rolling Pin

Age Group: Toddlers, Preschool, School Age

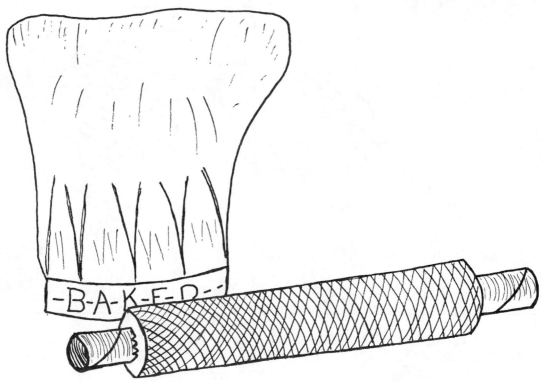

-B-A-K-E-R-

How To Use It:
Child wears baker's hat and may roll the rolling pin back and forth when making pretend pies and cookies. Soft modelling clay might be used as dough.

What It Does:
Encourages dramatic and role play of housekeeping and community jobs. Rolling the rolling pin uses grasping and large arm movements.

(Social & Emotional Process, Creative Process, Physical Development Process)

What You Need To Make It

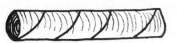
sturdy long thin
cardboard tube

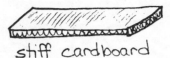
contact paper

scissors

masking
tape

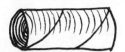
sturdy short wide
cardboard tube

stiff cardboard

white paper bag
(large enough to fit
over child's head)

nontoxic felt tip
marker

pencil

stapler

OR:

OR : wooden dowel, matte knife, tagboard, potato chip can or
other thin can and 2 plastic lids, white tissue paper,
crayons, etc.

How To Make It

① Trace the rim of the thin
tube on the stiff cardboard.
Next, trace the rim of the <u>wide</u>
tube <u>around</u> this circle. Now
trace another circle about 1½"
<u>larger</u> than the second circle.
  Repeat these directions
once again. ✳

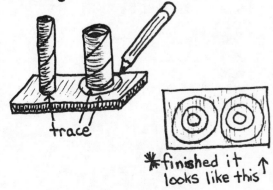
trace

✳finished it
looks like this↑

② Cut around the <u>largest</u> circles.
Cut slits around the outside
as shown.

cut

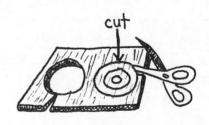

38

③ From the center to the smallest circle, cut slits like this: ✳.

cut

④ Put the thin tube through the wide tube. Push the circles onto the thin tube at each end.

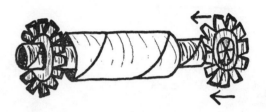

⑤ Fold the outside tabs of the circles over the ends of the wide tube and tape securely.

⑥ Cover the wide tube with contact paper.

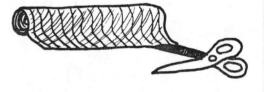

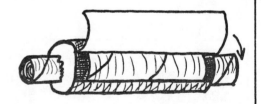

⑦ Cut a strip of cardboard about 2" wide, long enough to go around the child's head and <u>overlap</u> a few inches.

⑧ Staple the cardboard strip into a circle. Staple the open end of the bag to the inside of the cardboard rim. Write "BAKER" on the rim.

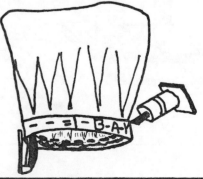

Colored Button Sort

Age Group: Preschool, School Age

How To Use It:

Young children match the colored tubes with the circle on the board of the same color. Older children then may fill the tubes with buttons of the same color. Adult may give directions like "fill the red tube", "Count the buttons in the blue tube", etc.

What It Does:

Teaches color matching and color naming. May also help with basic number understanding. Picking up buttons also uses fine finger skills.

(Cognitive & Symbolic Process, Physical Development Process)

What You Need To Make It

3 toilet paper rolls

small can & lid

contact paper of 6 different colors

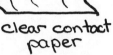

masking tape

clear contact paper

2 pieces of tagboard

pencil

lots of buttons (the same colors as the contact paper above)

scissors

OR: film canisters or aerosol can tops or any plastic or cardboard tubes, paint, crayons or markers and clear contact paper, any small "sort-able" objects: bottle caps, marbles, pen tops, etc.

How To Make It

① Trace 6 circles, the size of the tube rims, on a piece of tagboard. Cut out circles about ½" **bigger** than the tube rims.

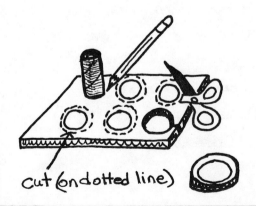

cut (on dotted line)

② Cut the circles as shown. Cut the toilet paper tubes in half. Tape the circles to one end of each tube.

circles
cut

tubes

cut

③ Cover each tube with a differently colored contact paper.

④ Cut out a circle of each contact paper - the size of a tube rim. Stick these circles to a piece of tagboard.

⑤ Cover the tagboard with clear contact paper.

⑥ Put the buttons in the can with the lid for storage.

Kazoo

Age Group: Preschool, School Age

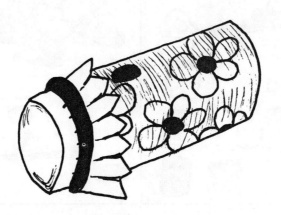

How To Use It:
Child hums or sings "do-do-do's into the open end of the tube, and a raspy, louder sound is heard. Kazoos can be played with other instruments, with other kazoos, or to songs. Two children might take turns copying each other's "kazoo rhythms."

What It Does:
Encourages musical expression, as well as listening and memory skills. Also uses tongue and lip movements used in speaking.

(Creative Process, Cognitive & Symbolic Process, Sensory & Perceptual Process)

What You Need To Make It

cardboard tube

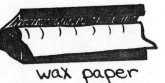
wax paper

colorful contact paper

thick rubber band

Scissors

OR: aluminum foil, crayons and clear contact paper, etc.

How To Make It

① Cut enough contact paper to go around the tube and <u>overlap</u> on one end about 1 inch. Cover the tube with the contact paper and fold the extra into the inside at one end

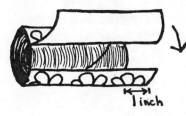
1 inch

② Cut wax paper a few inches larger than the tube rim.

④ Wrap the wax paper tightly around the end without the extra contact paper turned in, and put a rubber band around it to keep it on.

⑥ Cut a small hole (about ¼" diameter) with the scissors near the wax paper end of the tube.

hole

Musical Roller Pull Toy

Age Group: Toddlers, Preschool

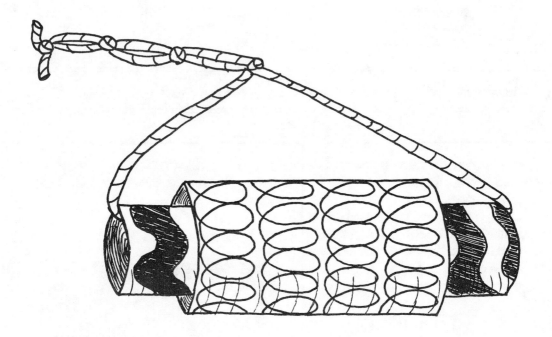

How To Use It:
Child pulls the rollers across the floor by the string. Bells inside the rollers make music as the toy is pulled.

(May also be used as a mobile for infants!)

What It Does:
Bright colors attract the child to the toy; pulling it encourages grasping and walking skills. The sounds of the bells encourage listening and help to keep the child's interest.

(Physical Development Process, Sensory & Perceptual)

What You Need To Make It

long, thin cardboard tube

sturdy string

colorful contact paper

short, wide cardboard tube

scissors

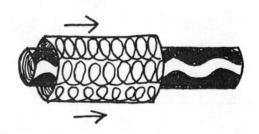
small bells

OR: wide & thin tin cans with no rough edges, thick yarn or cord, colored paper or news print and clear contact paper, etc.

How To Make It

① Cover each tube with differently colored contact paper.

② Slip the wider tube over the thin tube.

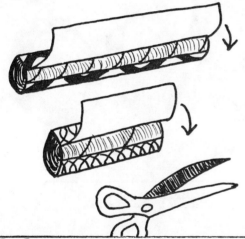

③ Cut a long piece of string. Put it through the long thin tube. Put the bells on the string so they are inside the long thin tube.

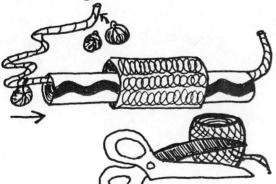

④ Tie the 2 ends of the string in a knot about 12 inches from the tubes. Tie the rest of the string in knots.

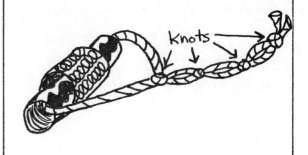

knots

Ring Catch

Age Group: Preschool, School Age

How To Use It:
Child holds the tied end of the long tube with the string and rings hanging down. By swinging the string and rings up, the child tries to catch the rings on the tube. Children may take turns with each other. For preschoolers, toy might be made with only 1 ring.

What It Does:
Uses hand-eye skills, as well as large arm movements.

(Sensory & Perceptual Process, Physical Development Process)

What You Need To Make It

 long thin sturdy cardboard tube

 colored contactpaper   scissors

  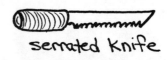

wide sturdy cardboard tube   masking tape   strong string   serrated knife

OR: dowel, rubber canning lids or plastic lids, glue or heavy tape, etc.

How To Make It

① With the knife, cut the <u>widest</u> cardboard tube into sections to make rings. (Cut as many as you wish.) Cut them ½" to 1" wide.

② Cover the rings and the long thin tube with contact paper.

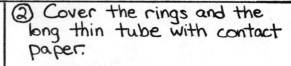
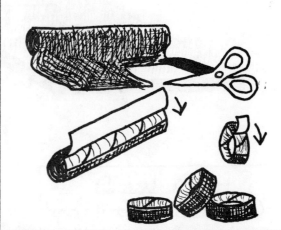

③ Cut a long piece of string. Tie one end of the string to one end of the long thin tube. Tie it tightly. Tape over it so it will stay securely.

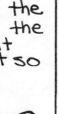
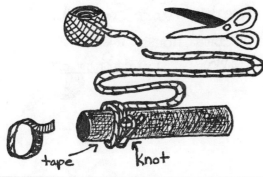

tape   knot

④ Put the wide rings on the string. Tie the end of the string to the last ring.

knot

Carpet Puzzles

Age Group: Infants, Toddlers, Preschool

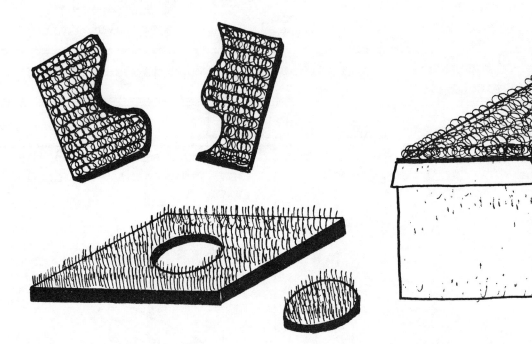

How To Use It:

Child pieces together the carpet shapes. With infants and toddlers, adult may hold up the puzzle and push out the middle piece in a "hide and seek" game. Crawlers and toddlers may then pick up the piece and hand it to the adult to begin again. With preschoolers, adult may discuss shapes and their names.

What It Does:

Encourages problem solving. Helps child become aware of different textures and shapes. Uses hand coordination skills. Also encourages play with other people.

(Creative Process, Sensory & Perceptual Process, Physical Development, Social & Emotional)

What You Need To Make It

pieces of clean carpet or carpet samples

glue

matte knife

piece of cardboard

cardboard box & lid

OR: tin snips, wooden board, cloth and tagboard, jacknife, etc.

How To Make It

① Use the cardboard as a cutting surface so you do not mar your table.
Cut the carpet with a matte knife to make puzzle pieces.

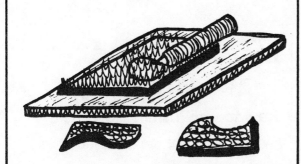

② For puzzles cut out of shag rug, put glue along the cut edges of all of the pieces. When dry, this keeps the threads from pulling out.

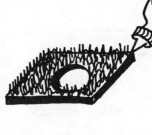

glue

③ Glue a piece of carpet on the lid of the box. Put the puzzles in the box for storage.

EASY GRASP BALL

AGE GROUP: INFANT, TODDLER

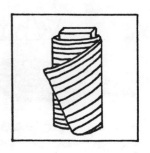

HOW TO USE IT:

The infant can easily grasp the ball by one of its "wedges". The ball can be pushed, tossed, or rolled back and forth with another person.

Lightly rub the infant's cheek with the differently textured wedges of the ball. Describe the colors and textures of the ball with toddlers.

WHAT IT DOES:

The ball, because it is easy for an infant to handle, encourages the development of hand and arm muscles.

The bright colors and different textures of the material help the child learn about the variations in the sensory world of seeing and touching. Discussion about the textures and colors helps older children learn word concepts.

(Physical Development, Sensory & Perceptual, Cognitive & Symbolic Processes)

WHAT YOU NEED TO MAKE IT:

12 - 7" x 6" scraps of fabric - bold colors and a variety of textures

OR tracing paper

OR old clean stockings

(sewing machine is handy but not necessary)

HOW TO MAKE IT:

① Trace these patterns with wax paper. Cut out the wax paper patterns.

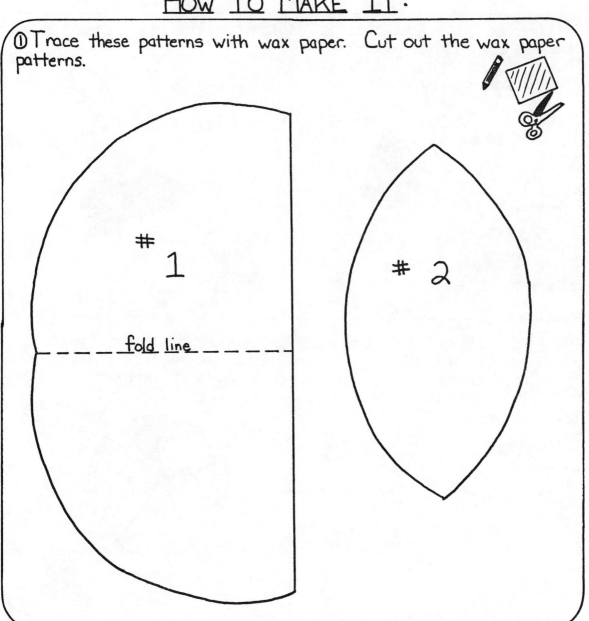

#1

fold line

#2

②Cut 12 of each pattern piece out of fabric.

③With right sides together, fold piece #1 in half. With <u>right sides together</u>, sew each piece #2 to the curved edges of its matching piece #1, using a ¼" seam.

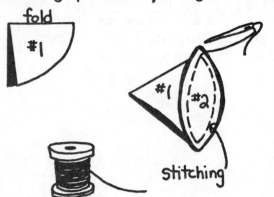

fold

#1

#1 #2

stitching

④Turn so the right side is facing out. Stuff each "wedge" with fiberfill through the remaining open seam.

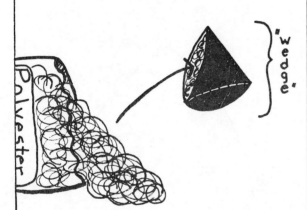

"wedge"

⑤Stitch the open seam closed.

NOTE! :These terms are used in directions ⑥-⑫:
"top" point
"side" point

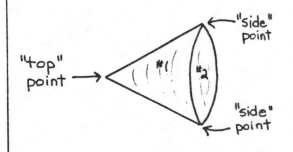

"side" point

"top" point →

#1 #2

"side" point

⑥Securely tack the "top" points (see NOTE at left) of 4 wedges together.

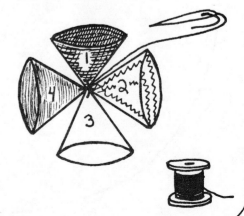

⑦ Forming them into a cross-like pattern, tack these 4 wedges together at one "**side**" point.

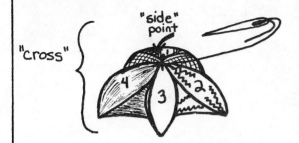

⑧ Repeat directions ⑥ and ⑦ with 4 <u>new</u> wedges to make a second "cross" section.

step ⑥

step ⑦

⑨ Tack the "top" points of the two "cross" sections together. (Where the "top" points meet will be the middle of the finished ball.)

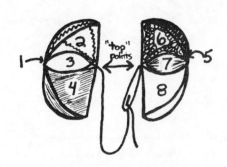

⑩ Tack each untacked "side" point of one "cross" section to an untacked "side" point of the other "cross" section.

⑪ Fitting them in between the "side" points of the two "cross" sections you just connected, tack the "top" point of each of the remaining 4 wedges to the middle of the ball.

(these two go on the other side of the ball)

⑫ Tack each untacked "side" point to the "side" points on either side.

You're done!

Fabric Matching Game

Age Group: Preschool, School Age

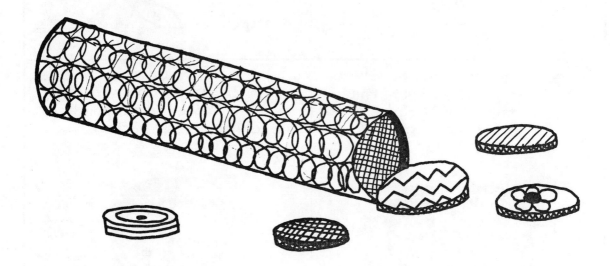

How To Use It:

Many different games are possible: the simplest is that the child empties the can and matches the 2 circles of each pattern that are the same. Adult may discuss "same" and "different."

Other traditional games: "go fish", bingo, concentration, etc.

What It Does:

Encourages visual matching and awareness of detail. Helps understanding of some basic concepts. Games encourage play with other children.

(Cognitive & Symbolic Process, Social & Emotional Process)

Another Way To Make & Use It:
Make the circles out of textured objects (as in the Feel & Tell Box). Child then tries to match the circles while blindfolded.

What You Need To Make It

tube potato chip container & lid   scraps of fabric   colorful contact paper   cardboard

sissors   glue

OR: any box, designs drawn on paper and clear contact paper, colored cardboard, materials as in "Feel & Tell Box", etc.

How To Make It

① Cut **2** circles (a little smaller than the size of the can) out of **each** kind of fabric.

② Cut circles of cardboard for each circle of fabric. Glue each fabric circle to a cardboard circle.

③ Cover the can with contact paper. Put the circles in the can.

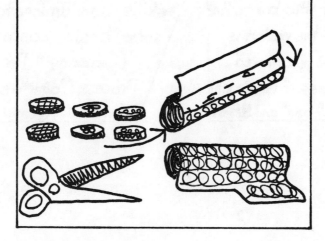

Feel & Tell Box

Age Group: Preschool, School Age

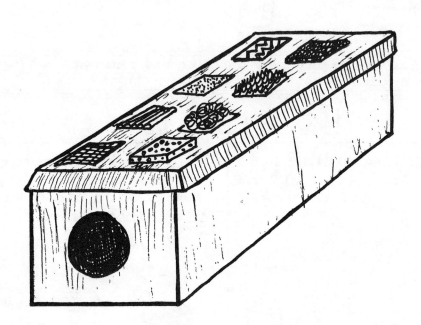

How To Use It:
Child puts one hand inside the box and feels one square of material. With the other hand, she or he then touches the squares on top of the box to find its match. When the match is found, the square is removed from the box to see if it is right. Adult may discuss "same" and "different".

What It Does:
Encourages child to identify by touch, and helps awareness of differences in textures. Encourages matching skills, and understanding of some basic concepts.
(Sensory & Perceptual Process, Cognitive & Symbolic Process)

What You Need To Make It

scraps of cloth, rug samples, steel wool, sandpaper, sponge, drinking straws, etc.

shoe box & lid

scissors

piece of cardboard

glue

nontoxic glue

<u>OR</u>: any material of different textures, any cardboard box & lid, matte knife, tagboard, etc.

How To Make It

① Cut 2 squares of each textured item.

② Glue <u>1</u> of each of these squares onto the shoe box lid.

③ Glue the other pieces onto squares of cardboard and put them in the box.

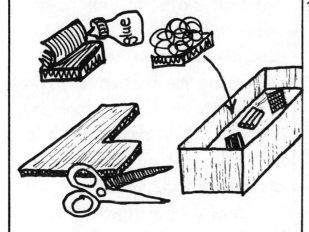

④ Cut a hole in one end of the shoe box large enough for a child's hand. Put on the lid.

Cut & remove

FOLLOWING FOOTSTEPS GAME

AGE GROUP: PRESCHOOL, SCHOOL AGE

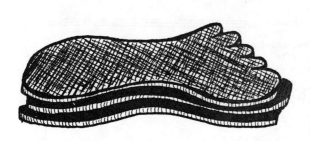 

HOW TO USE IT:

The feet are placed on the floor, close enough together so the children can hop or step from one to another. Children take turns rolling the dice and taking as many steps as the number that comes up. Children may count out-loud as they step, or name and match the foot they land on as right or left. The dice can be tossed from one child to another after each turn. Activities (jump rope, puzzle, etc.) can be placed next to some feet to be completed before the next turn.

Feet can also show children where to go for new activities.

WHAT IT DOES:

The game encourages play with others and taking turns. Hopping, stepping, tossing and catching all help to develop large muscle skills. The development of counting and matching skills, as well as an understanding of left-right concepts, are also encouraged.

Using the feet as paths to activities (or the bathroom, etc) gives the child direction while still allowing-and encouraging- a sense of independence.

(Social & Emotional, Physical Development, Cognitive & Symbolic, Creative Processes)

What You Need To Make It:

vinyl

OR rug samples,
felt, old shower
curtain, etc.

tracing
paper

OR wax paper

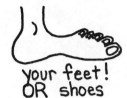

your feet!
OR shoes

pencil

ALSO: materials for dice
See "Milk Carton Blocks"

How To Make It:

① Trace your right and left feet on a piece of tracing paper with a pencil.

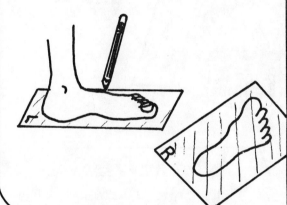

② Cut out the tracing paper feet. Using them as a pattern, cut out 20-30 vinyl feet (make as many as you want).
Make a dice as described in "Milk Carton Blocks".

Milking Cow

Age Group: Preschool, School Age

<u>How To Use It</u>:
Children can climb on it and sit on it, and older children may learn to "milk" it. Can be used in discussions about animals, farms, and where food products come from.
Help from an adult may be needed when milking.

<u>What It Does</u>:
Helps child become familiar with animals and how animals are useful to people. May be used in dramatic play. "Milking" uses fine finger movements.
(Social & Emotional Process, Creative Process, Physical Development Process)

<u>To"Milk"</u>: (it takes practice!) squeeze from the top of the fingers, nearest the hand part of the glove, <u>down</u> toward the fingertips. Water will come out through the holes in the fingertips.

What You Need To Make It

sturdy sawhorse

3 carpet pieces each at least 12" x 20"

strong twine or rope

old newspapers

large plastic pail

1 rubber glove

shoe box & lid

hammer

2 large nails

pin

colored contact paper

glue

colored construction paper

scissors

OR: 1 large carpet, burlap bags, any material to pad the saw horse, any oblong box, masking tape, etc.

How To Make It

① Wrap newspaper thickly around the sawhorse to pad it.

② Wrap the 3 carpet pieces over the newspaper. Wrap rope tightly around so the carpet stays firmly in place.

←newspaper

③ Cut eyes, eyelashes, horns, ears, nose and tongue out of construction paper.

eyelashes

eyes

horns

ears

nose

tongue

④ Glue these on the lid of the shoebox.

glue

⑤ Nail the bottom of the shoe box onto one end of the sawhorse.

⑥ Glue the lid securely onto the box.

glue

⑦ Cut 5 or 6 long pieces of rope and tie them onto the _other_ end of the cow for a tail.

tie

⑧ Make pin pricks in the fingertips of the rubber glove.

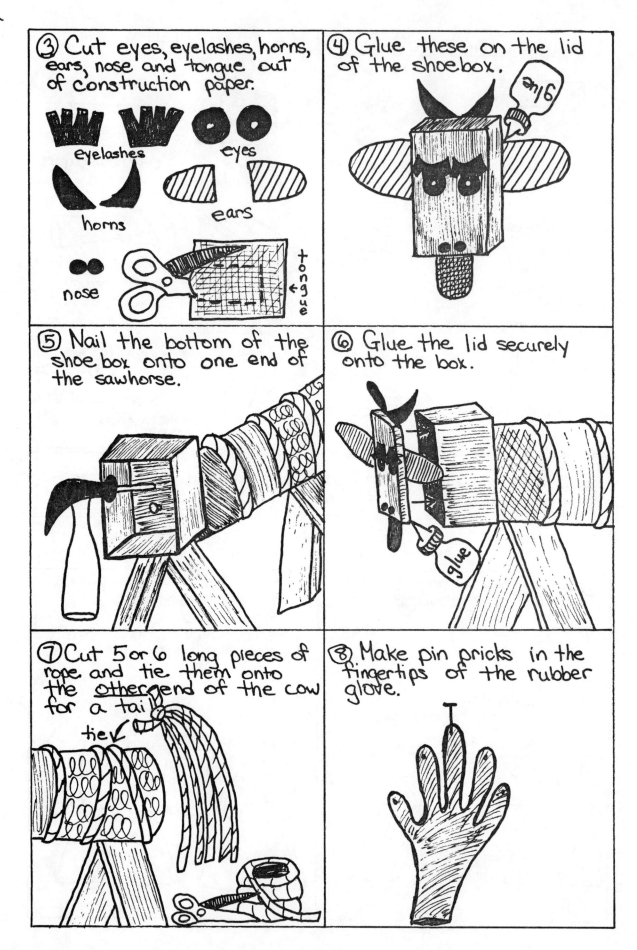

⑨ Fill the glove with <u>water</u>. Tie it at the top and attach it with rope to the bottom of the cow.

tie

⑩ Cut out the letters MILK in contact paper and put them on the plastic container. Put the container under the glove.

Stuffed Kick Toy

Age Group: Infant

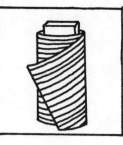

How To Use It:

For an infant or crawler, attach the ends of elastic to the crib sides so that the stuffed pillow is within kicking distance of the child.

When the baby outgrows this activity, the elastic can be removed and the pillow becomes a cuddle toy.

What It Does:

Bright colors attract the baby to the toy, and the facial features encourage an interest in looking at people.

Kicking encourages leg muscle development that will help later walking skills. It also develops a beginning awareness of cause and effect.

As a cuddle toy, it encourages fantasy play, and provides the child with comfort as well as practice in nurturing.

(Sensory & Perceptual, Physical Development, Cognitive & Symbolic, Creative, Social & Emotional Processes)

WHAT YOU NEED TO MAKE IT:

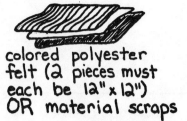

colored polyester felt (2 pieces must each be 12"x 12") OR material scraps

needle & thread (sewing machine is handy but not necessary)

2- 1½ foot long pieces of thick elastic

OR clean old pantyhose, pillow, etc.

HOW TO MAKE IT:

① Cut out 2 circles of felt, each about 1 foot in diameter.

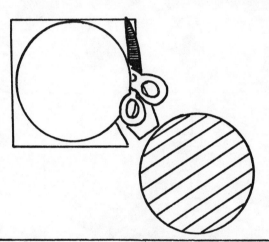

② Cut out facial features and sew them securely to one of the circles.

③ Sew each piece of elastic securely to opposite sides of the <u>other</u> circle.

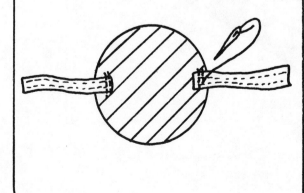

④ Sew the outsides of the circles together, <u>leaving a 3 inch opening.</u>

⑤Stuff with fiberfill until nice and fluffy.

⑥Sew the opening closed.

Texture Ball

Age Group: Infants, Toddlers

How To Use It:
Infant may touch and push the ball. As the child gets older, he or she may roll it back and forth with another person. Adult may discuss "soft" "smooth" and other words to describe the textures of the ball with older children.

What It Does:
Encourages touching and learning how textures differ. Encourages pushing and grasping skills. May help older children understand some word concepts.
(Sensory & Perceptual Process, Physical Development Process, Cognitive & Symbolic Process)

<u>What</u> <u>You</u> <u>Need</u> <u>To</u> <u>Make</u> <u>It</u>

 scraps of differently textured material: wool, cotton, vinyl, terrycloth, corduroy, etc.

 needle & thread

 scissors

 tracing paper

 pencil

 about 4 pairs of old clean stockings

<u>OR</u> waxed paper, sewing machine, clean rags or lint from a clothes dryer, etc.

<u>How</u> <u>To</u> <u>Make</u> <u>It</u>

① Trace the pattern on the next page with tracing paper and cut it out.

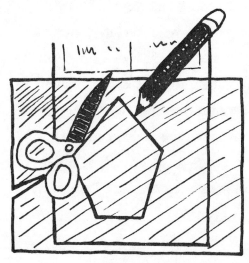

② Cut <u>12</u> of these out of the material scraps.

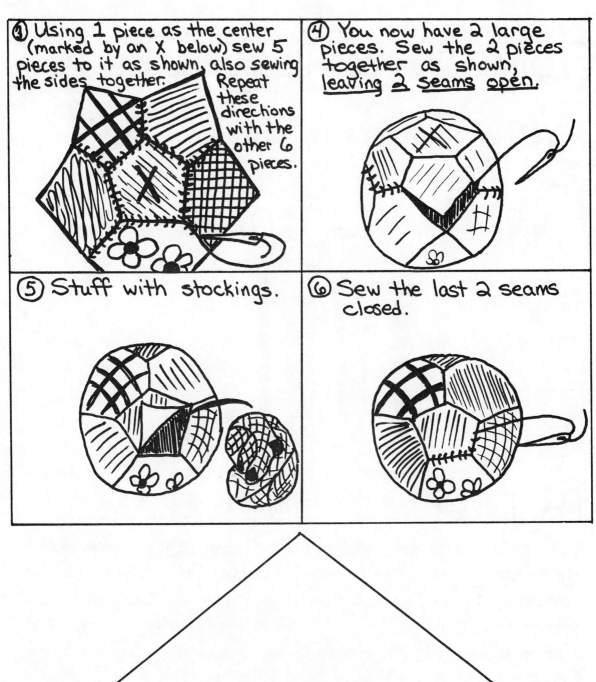

③ Using 1 piece as the center (marked by an X below) sew 5 pieces to it as shown, also sewing the sides together. Repeat these directions with the other 6 pieces.

④ You now have 2 large pieces. Sew the 2 pieces together as shown, leaving **2 seams open.**

⑤ Stuff with stockings.

⑥ Sew the last 2 seams closed.

trace this pattern

CLOTHESPIN MATCHING GAME

AGE GROUP: Toddler, Preschool, School Age

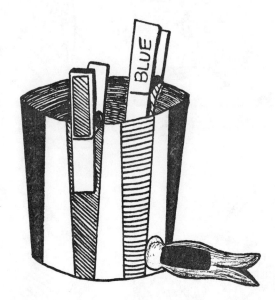

How To Use It:

The colors on the clothespins are matched to the colors on the container. (Color names can be written on one side of the clothespin for early schoolagers.) Count the clothespins; name the colors; find other objects that are the same or different colors. How many things can you think of that are the same colors as the clothespins? Let the child draw them!

Note: Use "slip-on" clothespins with children under the age of 2½-3 years.

What It Does:

This activity encourages matching and color naming, counting and reading skills, and the understanding of some basic word concepts. All of these skills are related to language development.

Using the clothespins helps to develop eye-hand skills and finger muscles.

(Cognitive & Symbolic, Physical Development Processes)

WHAT YOU NEED TO MAKE IT:

4 to 10 pincher clothes-pins (USE SLIP-ON CLOTHESPINS FOR YOUNG CHILDREN)

wide mouth plastic container and lid

4 to 10 colors of tape and matching felt·tip markers

HOW TO MAKE IT:

①Color both sides of each clothespin with a piece of colored tape. (For schoolagers, only cover one side with tape; write the color name on the other side with felt·tip marker.)

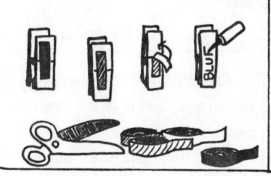

②Cut a piece of each tape, a little longer than the height of the container. Stick the tapes to the container so the tape goes over the top edge of the rim.

Store the clothespins inside!

VARIATIONS

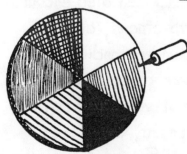

Color pie-shaped areas of cardboard circles to match the clothespin colors. Cover the cardboard with clear contact paper.

Cut a hole in the plastic container lid. Standing over the container, children try to drop the clothespins through the hole. Make a color-coded drop-through game with 2 or 3 colors and 2 or 3 containers!

ETC!

Box Camera

Age Group: Toddler, Preschool, School Age

How To Use It:

Children can draw or cut out pictures from magazines and paste them on squares of tagboard to be placed inside of the box. Real photos of each child can also be used.

Pictures can be removed from the box after the child "takes" a picture and counts to ten.

The camera can be used to help children get to know others in new groups. It can also be used in discussions about feelings, self-concept and identity topics, and in dramatic free play.

What It Does:

Cutting and drawing encourage creative expression and fine motor skills.

"Taking" pictures encourages dramatic play and counting skills. It can also encourage play with others, and can promote understanding and acceptance of self and others.

(Creative, Physical Development, Cognitive & Symbolic, Social & Emotional Processes)

What You Need To Make It:

cocoa can <u>with</u> <u>the</u> <u>label</u>
<u>still</u> <u>attached</u>
OR cardboard bandaid
box

hammer & nail

colored construction paper

tagboard

or cardboard

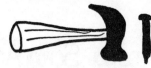

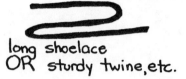

large <u>flat</u> button
OR threadspool,
wheel, etc.

long shoelace
OR sturdy twine, etc.

How To Make It:

① Punch a hole in the 2 narrow sides of the can with a hammer and nail.
(If the holes are sharp, be sure to file or sandpaper them smooth.)

2 holes

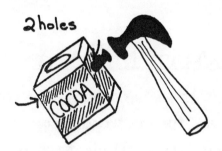

② Glue the construction paper over the can label.
Make a "lens" by gluing the button to the middle of one of the wide sides of the box.
(Stronger glue is sometimes necessary.)

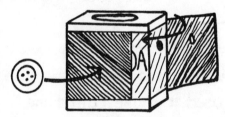

(Poke a hole through the construction paper for the 2 holes.)

③ String the shoelace through the 2 holes and tie securely so the camera can be worn around the neck.

Glue on decorations!

④ Cut out pictures from magazines, glue them onto square pieces of tagboard, and put them in the box.

Let the child draw pictures for the camera!

Styrofoam Bubble Boat

Age Group: Toddler, Preschool, School Age

EGG CARTON

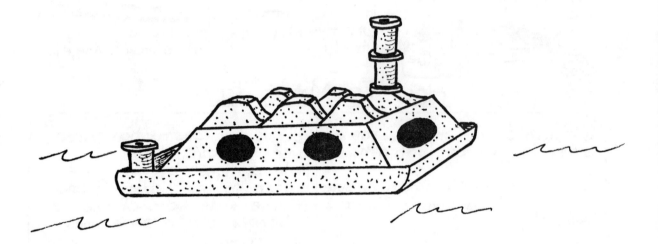

How To Use It:

The boat floats on water and can be used to make bath time more fun, or launched in sinks, puddles, etc.

Name and describe the boat with your child; make up stories to go with it.

With preschoolers and school-agers, discuss why it floats. What other objects might float? Try them!

What It Does:

By making bath time more fun, the boat encourages a positive attitude toward grooming skills.

It also encourages fantasy play and creative expression.

Both for children who live close to large bodies of water and for those who do not, toy boats can stimulate an interest in learning about water and transportation. It also helps them understand science principles of weight and flotation.

(Social & Emotional, Cognitive & Symbolic, Creative Processes)

WHAT YOU NEED TO MAKE IT:

styrofoam meat
or fruit tray

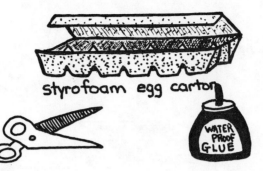

styrofoam egg carton

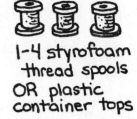

1-4 styrofoam
thread spools
OR plastic
container tops

HOW TO MAKE IT:

① Be creative! Using the meat tray as a base, glue assorted pieces of the styrofoam egg carton to it. Cut out windows; attach spools for smoke stacks, chocks (the hook up near the edge of the boat) etc. Plastic container tops add variety too. The ocean's the limit!

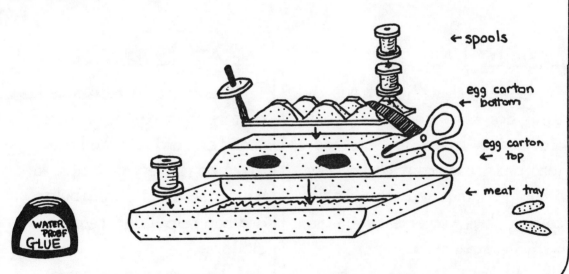

← spools

egg carton
← bottom

egg carton
← top

← meat tray

Because the boat is lightweight, it floats best in calm waters.

You can attach a 12" string to one end of the boat if it will be launched in large enough bodies of water for it to be pulled.

Think up other boat ideas! Make them out of wood, milk cartons, etc. Make sailboats...... ocean liners...... paddle boats...... tugboats...... barges............

MAIL SORTING GAME

AGE GROUP: PRESCHOOL, (EARLY) SCHOOL AGE

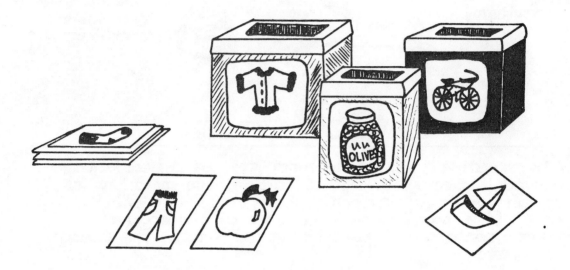

HOW TO USE IT:

Envelopes with pictures on them are sorted according to groups they belong to: clothes, food, and transportation (or any other groupings you can think of: colors, toys, objects beginning with the same sound, etc.).

As the child "mails" the pictures, describe and tell stories about the pictures together! Count how many are in each mailbox. What <u>other</u> objects can you and your child think of that belong in these categories?

WHAT IT DOES:

Learning to recognize how different things are grouped together, and how they are alike or different helps to build the child's vocabulary and can help later reading skills.

This game encourages creative expression, and "mailing" the envelopes gives the eyes and hands practice working together on fine-motor skills.

(Cognitive & Symbolic, Creative, Sensory & Perceptual Processes)

What You Need To Make It:

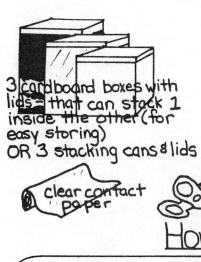

3 cardboard boxes with lids - that can stack 1 inside the other (for easy storing)
OR 3 stacking cans & lids

food box & can labels & old picture magazines

glue

12-18 old envelopes OR tagboard

clear contact paper

How To Make It:

① Cut out 4-6 pictures each of different kinds of food, transportation, and clothing from magazines and box and can labels.  	② Glue one picture for each category on a box. 
③ Cut a mailbox slit in the lid of each box, big enough for the envelopes. 	④ Glue the rest of the pictures on envelopes and cover with clear contact paper.  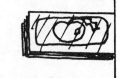   

FOAM BLOCK PUSH-THROUGH

AGE GROUP: INFANT, TODDLER, PRESCHOOL

FOAM RUBBER

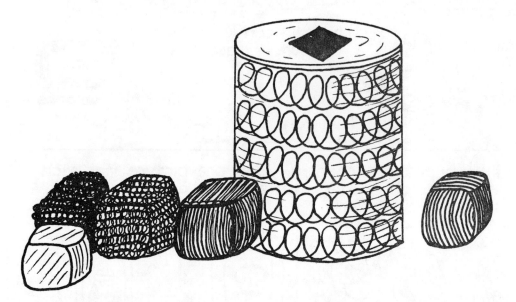

HOW TO USE IT:

Toddlers enjoy pushing the blocks through the hole in the top of the can, then opening the top and dumping them out.

Brush the infant's cheek or hand with the blocks! They can be left in the crib for the infant to grasp and feel.

Describe the different colors and textures with toddlers and preschoolers!

Blocks can be stacked and used in building play. They can also be thrown into the bucket (with the top off) or used in games of catch with other people.

WHAT IT DOES:

Push-through activities help eye-hand skills and help toddlers to better understand cause and effect relationships. The blocks give experience with many textures and colors, and discussions about them help to develop language skills. Grasping, building and throwing all encourage muscle development, and building games promote creative play. Block games with others promote social skills.

(Physical Development, Sensory & Perceptual, Cognitive & Symbolic, Social & Emotional, Creative Processes)

WHAT YOU NEED TO MAKE IT:

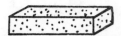

foam rubber: 2" thick
IMPORTANT: only
use foam that has
been marked
NONFLAMMABLE

washable, colorful
textured fabric
(corduroy, velveteen,
fake fur, dotted swiss,
etc.) Each piece at
least 7" x 9"

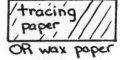

colorful contact paper

tracing paper
OR wax paper

large tin can
& plastic lid

needle & thread
(sewing machine is handy
but not necessary)

single edge
razor blade
OR saber saw

HOW TO MAKE IT:

① Cut the foam into 2" square cubes, using the razor blade. (You may wish to make other sizes too.)

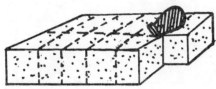

② Trace the pattern on the next page with tracing paper. Using this pattern, cut out fabric for each of the cubes.

③ Cover each block and stitch the seams. (If using a sewing machine: sew 3 sides, stuff with foam rubber, and finish by hand.)

④ Cover the tin can with colorful contact paper. Cut out a square 1¾" x 1¾" in the middle of the lid.

Store the blocks in the can!

TRACE THIS PATTERN

Remember to adjust the pattern if you are making blocks of different sizes.

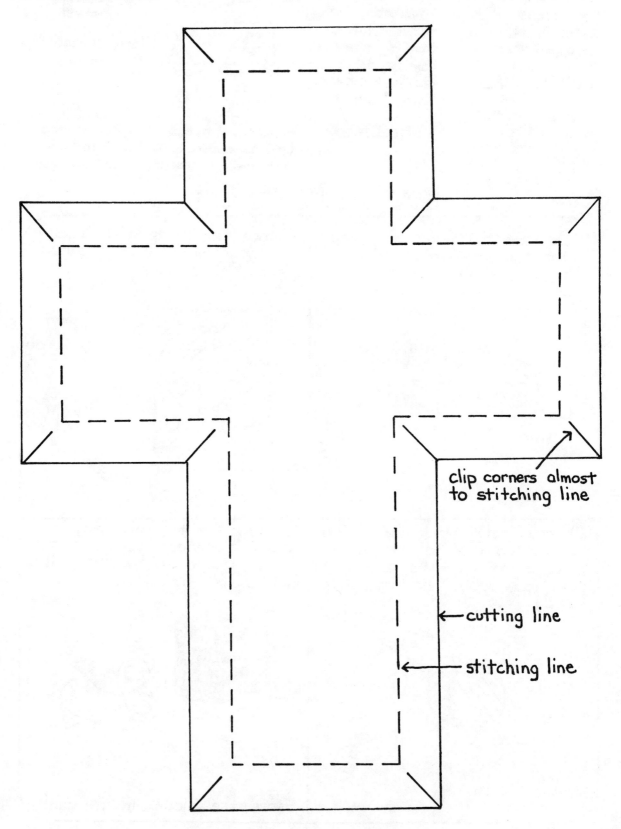

clip corners almost to stitching line

←cutting line

←stitching line

FINGER PUPPETS

AGE GROUP: INFANT*, TODDLER, PRESCHOOL, SCHOOL AGE

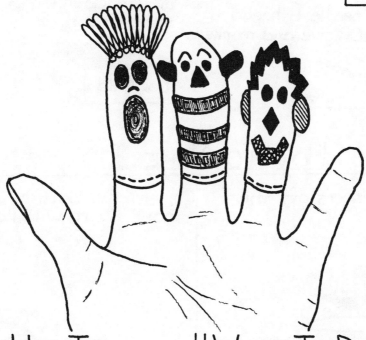

HOW TO USE IT:

Puppets are worn on fingers and are used in all kinds of creative dramatics. Toddlers who are beginning to talk can imitate the sounds of animals and people, or the puppets they wear might talk to the puppets of an adult or another child. Older children can act out stories that have been read to them, or they can make up their own plays. Be an enthusiastic audience!

* Adults wearing fingerpuppets can play hide and seek games with infants too!

WHAT IT DOES:

Puppets encourage children to express their ideas and their feelings, and by so doing, help to develop their confidence and their verbal skills.

Puppets encourage play with others, creativity, and the development of finger coordination.

(Creative, Cognitive & Symbolic, Physical Development, Social & Emotional Processes)

What You Need To Make It:

old glove

needle & thread
OR glue and markers

bits of cloth, fringe,
yarn, ribbon, etc.

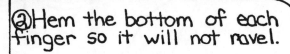

box & lid

How To Make It:

① Cut the fingers off the gloves.

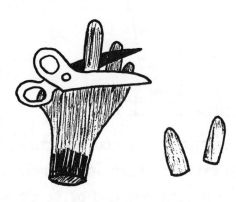

② Hem the bottom of each finger so it will not ravel.

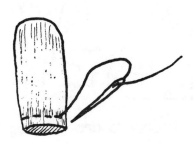

③ Sew on fringe, ribbon, etc. to make unique faces on each finger.

④ Store them in a box!

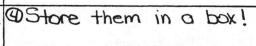

Lid Matching Puzzles

Age Group: Preschool, School Age

How To Use It:	What It Does:
Child picks a card and then uses the lids to copy the pictures on the card. The card may then be turned over to see if the lids and the card match. Child may play alone or take turns with others.	Encourages matching by color, shape, and/or size. May encourage play with others. (Cognitive & Symbolic Process, Social & Emotional Process)

What You Need To Make It

assorted clean
metal & plastic lids

shoe box & lid

nontoxic
felt tip
markers

unlined
index
cards

OR: any container large enough to store the game, crayons
or colored pencils, stiff white paper or tagboard and
scissors, assorted buttons, etc.

How To Make It

① On one side of each card, draw "picture directions" of how the lids could be arranged (by stacking them, lining them up in different orders, or putting small lids inside large lids.)

Directions for younger children should only use 2 or 3 lids per card. For older children, directions can be harder.

Be sure the color of the marker matches the color of the lid!

side 1

② On the other side of each card, draw a picture of how each picture direction would look when completed. Make 10-20 cards like this. Put the lids and the cards in the shoebox for storage.

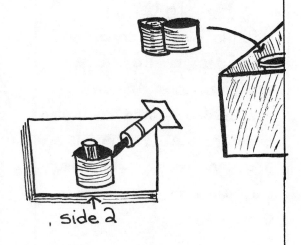

side 2

Lid Puppets

Age Group: Infants, Toddlers, Preschool, School Age

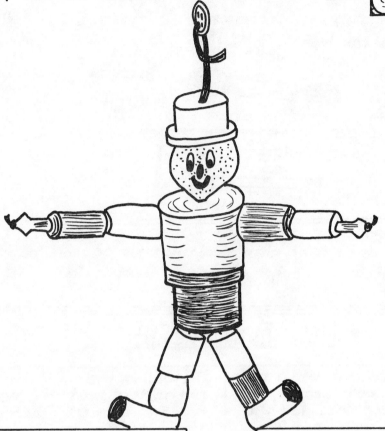

How To Use It:

Puppet can be bobbed up and down to "dance" on the elastic string, or used with other puppets to act out scenes. Older children may dress it with doll's clothes.

Puppet may be placed over crib for young infants to see, and later for them to pull and watch it bob.

What It Does:

For older children, the puppet encourages dramatic play, helps child become aware of body parts, and can encourage dressing skills.

For younger children, the colors and movement attract them to the toy, and encourage reaching and grasping.

(Creative, Social & Emotional, Sensory & Perceptual, Physical Development Processes)

What You Need To Make It

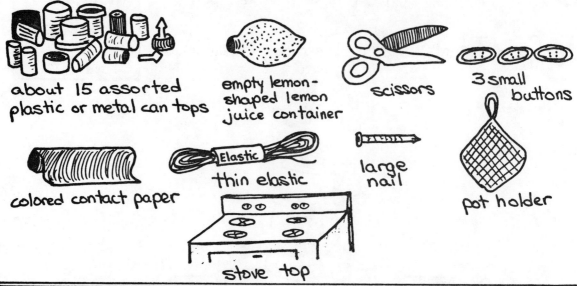

about 15 assorted plastic or metal can tops

empty lemon-shaped lemon juice container

scissors

3 small buttons

colored contact paper

thin elastic

large nail

pot holder

stove top

OR: thread spools or cardboard tubes and containers, rubber ball, small caps or dish soap nozzles or more buttons, bunsen burner or hot plate, or electric drill or scratch awl, etc.

How To Make It

① Lay the caps out on a table in the shape of a person, using the wider caps for the trunk and thinner caps for arms and legs.

② Holding the nail with the potholder, heat the nail over a stove burner. Then with the hot nail, melt 2 holes in the <u>top</u> of the <u>bottom</u> trunk cap.
Melt 2 holes on the <u>sides</u> of the <u>upper</u> trunk cap.
Melt 1 hole on the <u>side</u> of each foot cap as shown.

feet

holes

bottom trunk cap

upper trunk cap

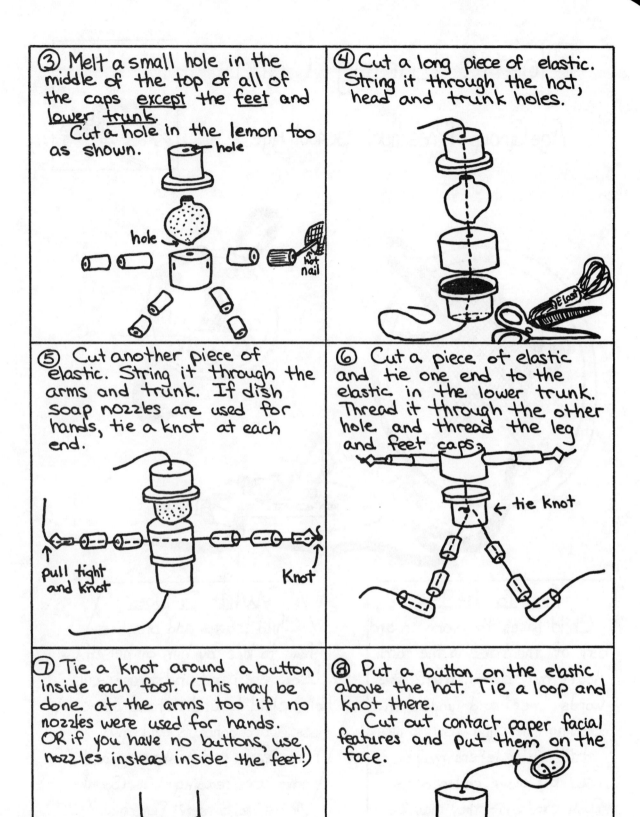

③ Melt a small hole in the middle of the top of all of the caps __except__ the __feet__ and __lower trunk__.
  Cut a hole in the lemon too as shown.

hole

hole →

hot nail

④ Cut a long piece of elastic. String it through the hat, head and trunk holes.

Elast

⑤ Cut another piece of elastic. String it through the arms and trunk. If dish soap nozzles are used for hands, tie a knot at each end.

↑ pull tight and knot

Knot

⑥ Cut a piece of elastic and tie one end to the elastic in the lower trunk. Thread it through the other hole and thread the leg and feet caps.

← tie knot

⑦ Tie a knot around a button inside each foot. (This may be done at the arms too if no nozzles were used for hands. OR if you have no buttons, use nozzles instead inside the feet!)

⑧ Put a button on the elastic above the hat. Tie a loop and knot there.
  Cut out contact paper facial features and put them on the face.

Plastic Lacing Cards

Age Group: Preschool, School Age

How To Use It:
Child laces the yarn in and out of the holes in the card. Adult may demonstrate the words "over" and "under" in showing the child how to lace.

Lids with letters may be used by older children as flash cards, or they may be used to spell words.

What It Does:
Child learns and practices how to lace by him or herself. Uses eye-hand and finger skills. Helps child to understand some basic word concepts and may help teach letter shapes and other pre-reading skills. (Social & Emotional, Sensory & Perceptual, Cognitive & Symbolic, Physical)

What You Need To Make It

plastic lids   thick yarn   colored contact   scissors
                                paper

paper punch   glue
                glue

OR: pieces of plastic bottles, cardboard and clear contact paper, shoe laces, etc.

How To Make It

① Cut out simple designs (or the letters of the alphabet) from contact paper.	② Put one design or letter on each plastic lid.
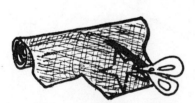	
③ Punch holes around the contact paper, either following the outline of the design, OR just in a circle.	④ Cut a long piece of yarn. Put nontoxic glue on each end. (This will make the ends stiff when they dry.)
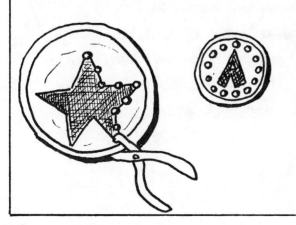	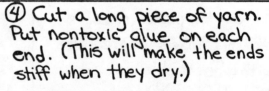 glue only the ends 

Rhythm Shakers

Age Group: Infants, Toddlers, Preschool, School Age

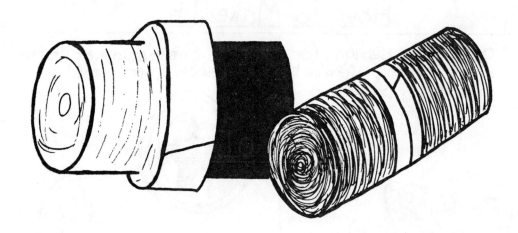

How To Use It:
Shaker rattles as it is moved. It can be pushed, rolled, or shaken. (Shakers may be filled with different objects, making different sounds.) Older children may shake it to music. Preschool & School Age children may compare weights of different containers and discuss concepts like "heavier," "lighter."

What It Does:
Encourages listening and learning how sounds can differ. Also encourages pushing, grasping and shaking movements. Encourages music and rythm expression. May help understanding of some basic weight concepts. (Sensory & Perceptual, Creative, Physical Development, Cognitive & Symbolic Processes)

<u>What</u> <u>You</u> <u>Need</u> <u>To</u> <u>Make</u> <u>It</u>

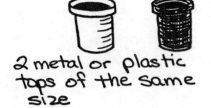  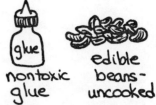

2 metal or plastic tops of the same size   adhesive tape   scissors   nontoxic glue   edible beans- uncooked

<u>OR</u>: plastic bottles and tops, any "noisy" food: peas, corn, etc., buttons or bells (tie these together so if the container opens, the bells or buttons are too big to be swallowed.)

<u>How</u> <u>To</u> <u>Make</u> <u>It</u>

① Put the beans inside one top.

② Put the second top over the first top. Glue and let dry, then tape them together securely.

Wagon

Age Group: Toddlers, Preschool, School Age

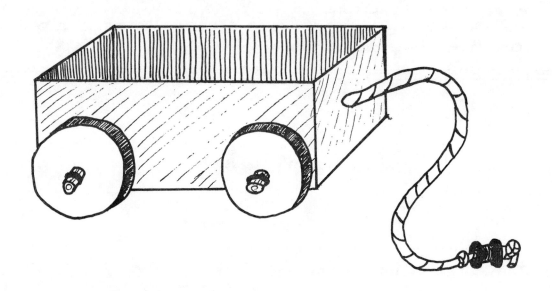

<u>How To Use It:</u>
Child may place objects in the box and pull it by the rope.

<u>What It Does:</u>
Encourages dramatic play and walking skills.

(Creative Process, Physical Development Process)

What You Need To Make It

4 plastic lids of the same diameter

Shoe box

2 dowels: 2" <u>longer</u> than the shoe box width

8 rubber bands

2 thread spools

pencil

2-3 feet of rope

scissors

glue

glue

<u>OR</u>: 4 metal lids and hammer and nail, paper fasteners, any box or can or plastic container, 2 pencils, 2 buttons or small lids, etc.

How To Make It

① Cut a hole in the middle of each lid – a <u>little</u> bigger than the size of the dowels.	② Trace around the circumference of the dowel on the 2 sides of the box as shown. Then cut a ✳ inside each circle.
	cut 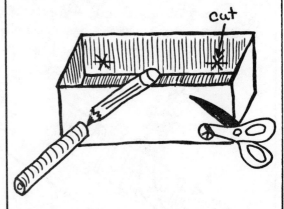

③ Push the 2 dowels through the star cuts. Glue the dowels to the box at the meeting points.

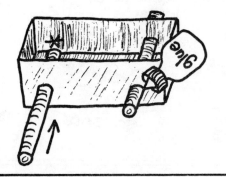

④ Wrap a rubber band tightly on the ends of each dowel, near the box.
Then put on a lid and another rubber band. Glue the rubber bands to the dowel.

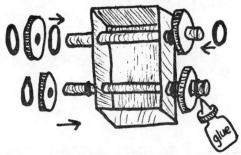

⑤ Cut a hole near the top of one of the short ends of the box.

⑥ Put the rope through this hole.

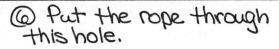

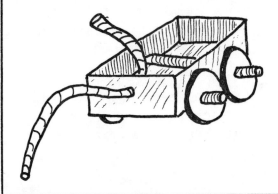

⑦ On the end of the rope inside the box, slip a thread spool onto the rope and tie a knot.

⑧ At the end of the rope outside the box, tie a knot about 3" from the end, slip a thread spool onto the rope and tie another knot.

Picture Puzzle

Age Group: Toddler, Preschool, School Age

How To Use It:

The child fits the puzzle pieces together to make a design.

Describing the colors and shapes of the pieces as the puzzle is being assembled can be fun! Names and uses of the objects in the finished picture can also be discussed. Make up stories to fit the pictures!

What It Does:

Puzzles encourage problem solving and learning how parts can be fitted together to make a whole. They also help the child learn about shapes and colors.

Puzzles help to develop hand and finger coordination skills. Talking about the puzzles encourages creativity, the understanding of many word concepts, and social skills.

(Creative, Cognitive & Symbolic, Physical Development, Sensory & Perceptual, Social & Emotional Processes)

WHAT YOU NEED TO MAKE IT:

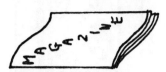

old picture magazines
OR see next page

OR cardboard

OR large envelope

clear contact paper

glue

HOW TO MAKE IT:

① Cut out a picture from a magazine.

② Glue it to tagboard and cover with clear contact paper.

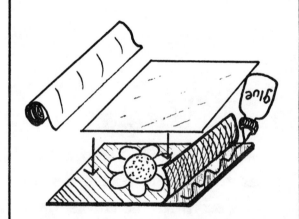

③ Cut it into puzzle pieces. (Numbers can be written on repetitious pieces)

④ Store it in a box. (If possible, glue or draw a picture of the finished puzzle on the cover.)

VARIATIONS

MORE Puzzle Ideas:

LABELS from food cans or boxes
kids' DRAWINGS
PICTURES traced from anywhere
ROAD MAPS (for schoolagers)
ETC.

✳ Lacing cards can be made by making holes with a paper punch all around the outside edge of a picture. See "Plastic Lacing Cards" in the first part of the book.

✳ For very young children (younger than about 2½ years) an outside boundary for the puzzles helps, or they'll get frustrated. (Older children often find outside boundaries helpful, too.)
Here are three ways of making a boundary:

Make the puzzle out of 2 pieces of cardboard or tagboard; use the basic instructions for "Matching Puzzles".

OR: Trace the puzzle shapes with a felt-tip marker on the bottom of a shallow cardboard box or a clean styrofoam meat tray. This will show how they fit together.

OR: If the puzzle is smaller than the box, glue a yarn outline of the puzzle to the inside of the box. This keeps the pieces from sliding around in the box as the child puts the puzzle together.

※ Puzzle pieces can each be a part of a whole picture (like a <u>leg</u> piece and an <u>arm</u> piece).....

<u>OR</u> they can be random shapes!

※ For YOUNGER children, a few large pieces are best:

Smaller pieces can be cut for older kids.

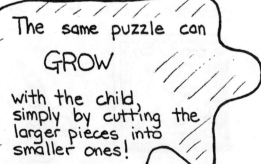

The same puzzle can

GROW

with the child, simply by cutting the larger pieces into smaller ones!

Milk Carton Blocks

Age Group: Infant, Toddler, Preschool, School Age

How To Use It:

Blocks are versatile and can be used in many different ways at many different ages: for building and stacking, counting, or as "cargo" on trucks or trains, etc. Objects can be placed inside to turn them into rattles or music makers for rhythm bands. Tall blocks can be numbered and knocked down like bowling pins with a foam or pom-pom ball. Beginning with a toddler's four or five large blocks, more blocks of different sizes and shapes can be added to the child's collection as she or he grows.

What It Does:

Building and stacking encourage a familiarity with shapes and sizes, and problem-solving about how they can be put together. They also help to develop hand coordination and are great tools for creative expression. Many block tasks encourage play with other children. Counting and comparing sizes and shapes (taller, shorter, etc.) encourages understanding of basic word concepts.

(Physical Development, Cognitive & Symbolic, Sensory & Perceptual, Social & Emotional, Creative Processes)

WHAT YOU NEED TO MAKE IT:

2 washed cardboard milk cartons of the same size for each block
OR any 2 sturdy boxes

 colorful contact paper
OR scotch tape, white paper, crayons and clear contact paper

HOW TO MAKE IT:

① Cut off the top of each of the 2 milk cartons at the same place.
(If making more than one block, cut different heights for differently sized blocks!)

Save the tops for other projects!

② Turn one carton bottom over and slip it into the other box.

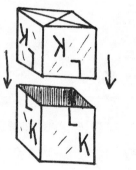

finished

③ Either cover the block with colorful contact paper, OR wrap it (like you would a package) with white paper and tape the edges.

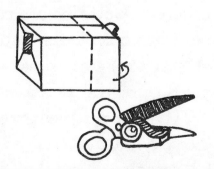

④ If you wrapped the block with white paper, now draw a number, shape or design on each side of the block and cover it with clear contact paper.

Other Ways To Make It & Use It:

Make a block with a height equal to the width.

Cover it with white paper and draw dots to make a <u>dice</u> for use in board games.
Draw 1 to 3 dots on each side for young children,
1 to 6 for older children.

Put bells, beans, jar lids, etc. inside to make a <u>rattle</u>.
Close securely with contact paper. It may be used as a rattle for infants or as a music maker for older children.

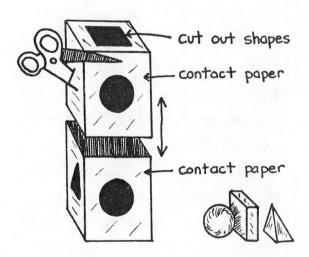

— cut out shapes

— contact paper

— contact paper

Cover each of the open cartons with contact paper and let the block be a <u>pull-apart toy</u> for the child to open and close.

Shapes can be cut in the sides; these help the child pull the cartons apart and can be used as <u>"drop-through" holes</u> for shape sorting games.

✳ the sky's the limit ✳ etc. ✳ etc. ✳ etc. ✳

SLIDING EGG

AGE GROUP: INFANT, TODDLER, PRESCHOOL

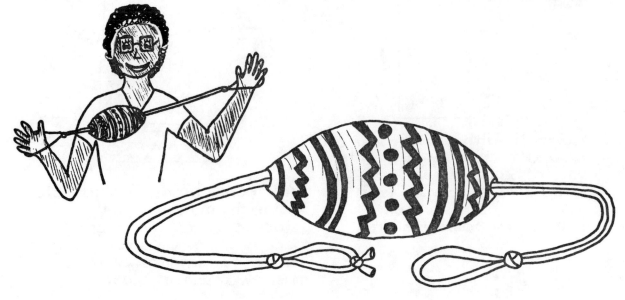

HOW TO USE IT:

The child holds a loop of the cord in each hand so that the "egg" can slide back and forth between the child's hands. An infant can watch an adult slide it back and forth.

The cord can also be tied to opposite sides of a crib, and the egg becomes a colorful kick toy (see the "Kick Toy" description).

WHAT IT DOES:

The colors and movement appeal to the young child's interest in change, and this toy lets the child experiment with making the movement happen by him or herself. This encourages a beginning awareness of cause and effect relationships. It helps to develop eye and arm muscles, and eye-hand coordination skills. As a kick toy it encourages leg muscle development.

(Sensory & Perceptual, Cognitive & Symbolic, Physical Development Processes)

103

What You Need To Make It:

 newspapers

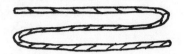 4' strong nylon cord OR sturdy string

 roundish balloon

 knitting needle

 non-toxic paint & brush

 matte knife OR paring knife

measuring cup

 water

dish pan OR pail

 XXXX FLOUR XXXX / wall paper paste OR white glue, any H_2O-soluble glue

How To Make It:

① Make a paste-like mixture of flour, water, and wallpaper paste in the dishpan.

 water

② Tear the newspapers into strips.

 NEWSPAPER

③ Blow up the balloon. Tie a knot.

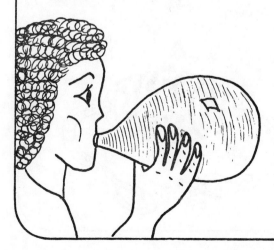

④ Paper mâche the balloon (about ¼" thick) by covering it with strips of newspaper that have been dipped into the pasty mixture. Let it dry thoroughly.

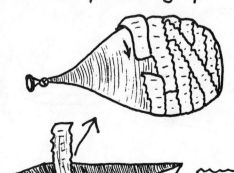

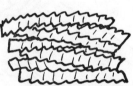

⑤ Paint the "egg" with bright colors and let it dry.

⑥ Cut 2 holes in opposite sides of the egg with the knife. Make each hole about the size of a nickel.

hole

hole

⑦ Tie one end of the cord to the end of the knitting needle.

⑧ Thread the knitting needle and cord through the egg twice.

⑨ Untie the cord from the knitting needle and knot the 2 ends together securely.

⑩ Tie knots large enough to keep the cord from slipping out of the egg on both ends as shown.

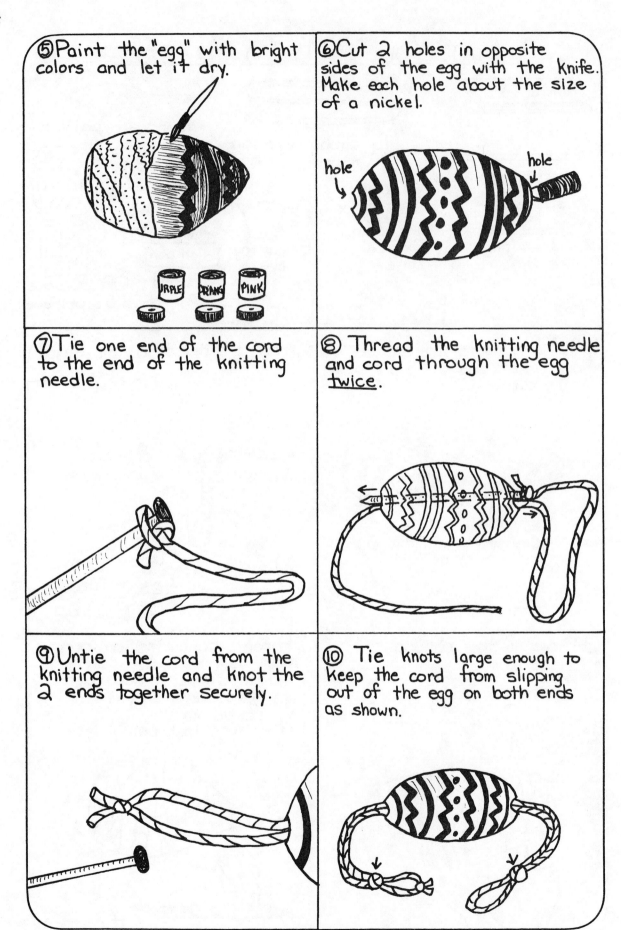

BACK PACK AND SIT-UPON

AGE GROUP: PRESCHOOL, SCHOOL AGE

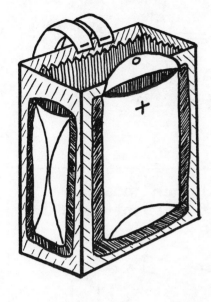

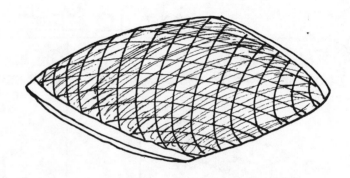

HOW TO USE IT:

The child puts the straps of the backpack over her or his shoulders, and wears it for dramatic play, and for carrying lightweight objects or found treasures on walks.

The sit-upon makes a waterproof pillow for outdoor and dramatic play use.

These toys can encourage discussions about camping, nature, hiking, mountains, and other interesting topics!

WHAT IT DOES:

It encourages creative play. Wearing it when taking walks allows and encourages taking responsibility for possessions. Through discussion, these toys also encourage learning about a number of concepts about our world.

(Creative, Cognitive & Symbolic, Social & Emotional Processes)

What You Need To Make It:

large grocery bag

manilla envelope

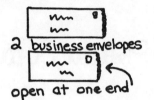 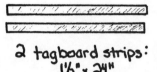
2 business envelopes
open at one end

old newspapers OR stockings, pillow, foam pellets, etc.

masking tape

scissors

2 tagboard strips: 1½" x 24"

2 large ziplock plastic bags

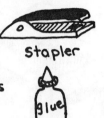
stapler

glue

How To Make It:

① Fold 2 or 3 inches of the bag rim to the inside.

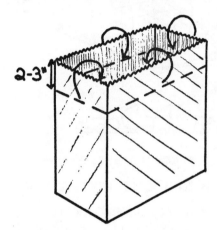

2-3"

② Glue and then tape the envelopes to the front and sides of the bag.

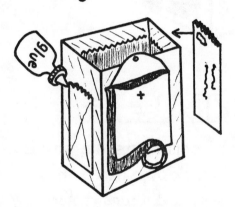

glue

③ Staple the cardboard strips to the bag: toward the center at the inside top, and near the outside edges at the bottom. (Check to make sure it fits the child so it can be easily put on and off.)

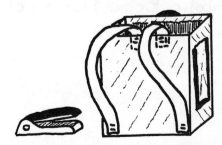

Decorate the pack!

SIT · UPON

① Shred the newspaper. (Kids often enjoy helping with this step.)

DAILY NEWS

② Put the shredded newspaper in one plastic bag until it is well stuffed.

③ Close the bag and slip the other bag over it, open end first.

opening end

④ Tape the opening for double durability.

MAIL CARRIER'S CAP AND BAG

AGE GROUP: PRESCHOOL, SCHOOL AGE

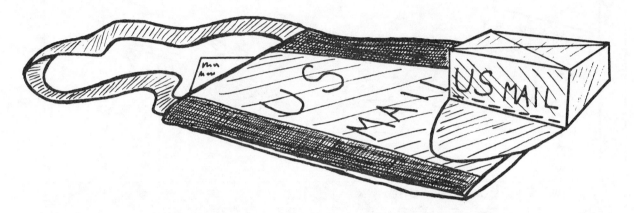

HOW TO USE IT:

A child can wear them for dramatic and role play, alone or with other children.

Encourage the child to write his or her own letters to deliver!

They can be used to encourage discussions about jobs, writing letters, where mail comes from, transportation (air mail, etc.) and other related topics.

The cap and bag are good companions for the "Mail Sorting Game."

WHAT IT DOES:

The cap and bag encourage dramatic play, as well as learning about and role playing people in their jobs. They also encourage social experiences with other children.

Discussions and role playing also encourage an awareness of, and an interest in, the uses of writing and a variety of concepts about communication, distance, etc.

(Creative, Social & Emotional, Cognitive & Symbolic Processes)

WHAT YOU NEED TO MAKE IT:

sandwich-size
paper bag

OR any size bag
that fits on
the child's head

grocery-size
paper bag

scissors

masking tape

stapler

VIOLET

crayon
OR felt tip pen, etc.

HOW TO MAKE IT:

① Cut off the top half of the sandwich bag. Fold in the edges of the bottom half to make it about 3 inches high.

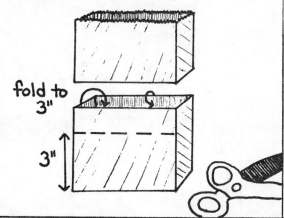

fold to 3"

3"

② From the top half of the sandwich bag, cut a semi-circle for a visor.

(flattened out)

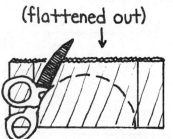

③ Staple the straight edge of the visor to one open side of the bottom half of the bag.

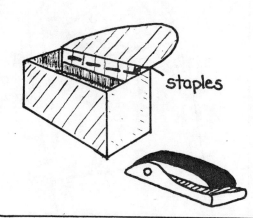

staples

④ Cut 4 inches off the rim of the grocery bag. Cut it once to make a long strip.

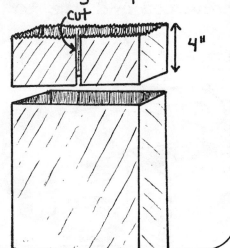

cut

4"

⑤ Fold the 4 inch strip in half _lengthwise_.

⑥ Fold in about 1 inch along the rim of the grocery bag.

1"↕

⑦ Flatten the bag and staple the sides as shown. The bottom of the bag becomes a front pocket!

pocket!

⑧ Staple the strip to each side of the bag to make a shoulder strap.

⑨ Cover the sharp staple edges with tape. (on both the cap and the bag.)

⑩ Decorate the cap and bag with crayon.

U VIOLET

✳ use old letters and envelopes for mail!

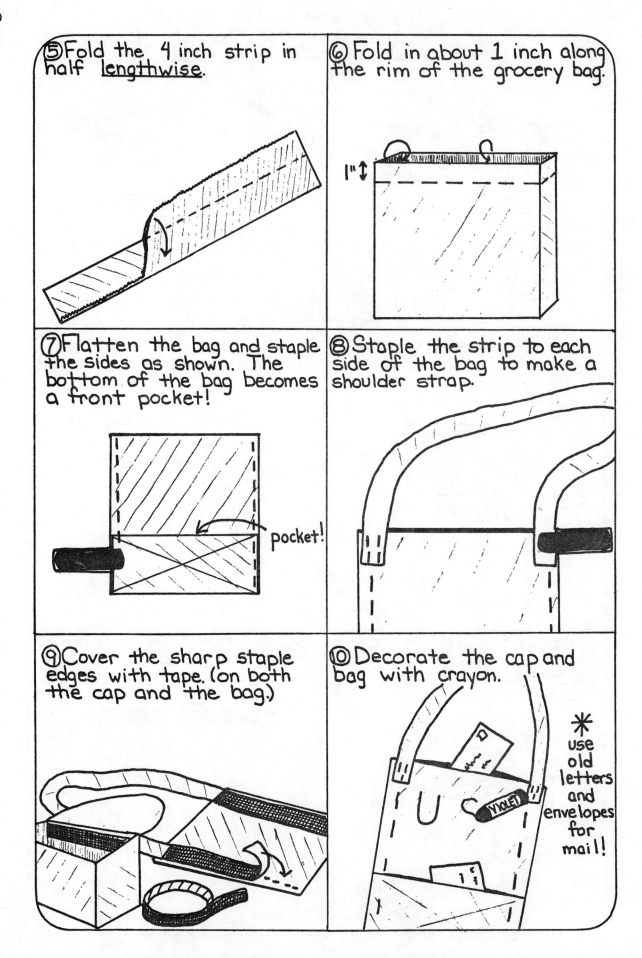

Bug Keeper

Age Group: School Age

How To Use It:

Child finds insects and puts insect, plants and food in container. (After a day or two, let the insect free.) Child might be encouraged to find out more about the insect, take responsibility for feeding, and with adult may discuss how insects are the same & different from other living things.

What It Does:

Helps child learn about and respect other living things; may help overcome fear of bugs. May encourage child to use books and/or other people to learn more about interesting things in their environment.

(Cognitive & Symbolic Process, Social & Emotional)

What You Need To Make It

bleach bottle, washed well

scissors

clean old stocking or pantyhose

2 sturdy rubber bands

OR: plastic ice cream tub or plastic pail, cardboard oatmeal box with or without lid, elastic or "twistem", etc.

How To Make It

① Cut around the bleach bottle just below the handle. (Save the top for other toy projects!)

cut →

② Cut out 4 "windows" in the sides.

③ Slip the bottle inside the stocking. Cut off the feet of the stocking so both ends are open, leaving at least 6" at each end.

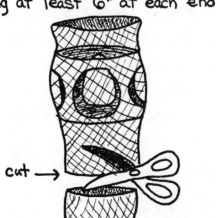

cut →

④ Gather the stocking to one side at the bottom, and fasten it securely shut with a rubber band. Fasten the top with a rubber band when a bug is found.

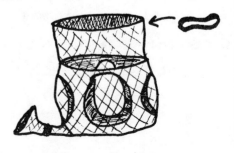

Face Masks

Age Group: Preschool, School Age

 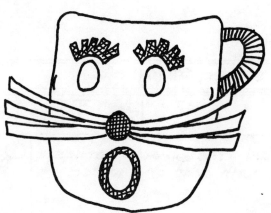

How To Use It:
Child slips mask over head and wears the mask over her or his face.

What It Does:
Encourages dramatic play, as well as encouraging play with other children.

(Creative Process, Social & Emotional Process)

What You Need To Make It

2 bleach bottles

colored contact paper

thick elastic

needle & strong thread

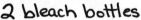
scissors

dish soap.

OR: stapler, string, etc.

How To Make It

① Wash the bleach bottles well with soap and water.

② Cut out a mask shape from the bottles. (1 design is included here - use your imagination and create others!)

cut

③ Cut 2 small holes at each side of the masks.

④ Cut elastic to go from one set of holes to the other.

⑤ Sew the elastic to the masks through the holes.

⑥ Cut strips of plastic from the cut up bottle to make whiskers. Round the edges.

⑦ Cut two slits in the middle of the mask and "weave" the whiskers through them. Cut holes for eyes and mouth.

⑧ Make exaggerated facial parts by cutting out eyelashes, etc. from contact paper. Put them on the masks.

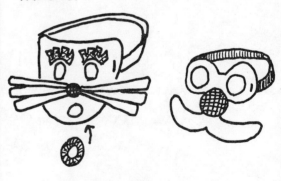

This is only 1 idea. Make up your own designs too! (Round all edges so they are not sharp.)

To use, trace with tracing paper or wax paper. Cut out the design on the tracing paper.* Then trace it on the plastic bottle.

*Before tracing it onto the bottle, you may wish to check to see if this design is the right size for your child. Using this as a basic pattern, you may make it larger or smaller to fit your child.

"Fish Bowl" Shaker Bottle

Age Group: Infants, Toddlers, Preschool

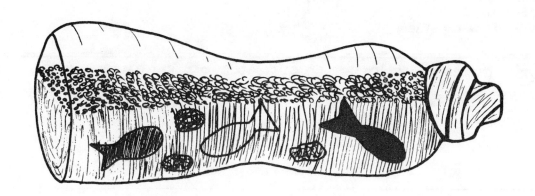

How To Use It:

Child may roll it or shake it. The water and objects move, and the vegetable oil forms bubbles that come to the top after shaking.

May be used in discussions with school age children about concepts such as "heavier" (the water) and "lighter" (the oil.)

What It Does:

Bright colors attract the child to the toy; the movement keeps the child's attention. Also encourages grasping and shaking skills. May be used in teaching basic weight concepts (Sensory & Perceptual Process, Physical Development Process, Cognitive & Symbolic Process)

What You Need To Make It

see-through plastic bottle and unopened top *

food coloring

water

vegetable oil

empty white or colored plastic bottle

adhesive tape

scissors

aluminum foil

(*baby oil jars with flip tops do not work well – they will not stay glued)

nontoxic glue

OR: pieces of colored plastic lids or containers, etc.

How To Make It

① Fill the see-through plastic bottle about ⅔ full with water.

② Add a few drops of food coloring to the water.

③ Add a little vegetable oil to the colored water.

④ Cut out plastic fish from empty plastic bottles. Make them small enough to fit in the first bottle.
Put them in it.

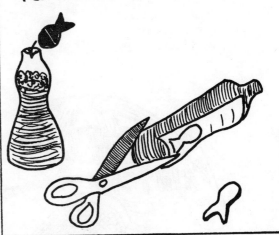

⑤ Roll pieces of aluminum foil into balls and other shapes and put them in the bottle.

⑥ Using nontoxic all purpose glue, glue and then securely tape the top of the bottle so it will not open.

Painter's Visor, Pail, & Roller

Age Group: Toddler, Preschool, School Age

How To Use It:
Child wears visor on his or her head. Fill the paint bucket with water and the child may then "paint" outside doors or walls with the paint roller.

What It Does:
Encourages dramatic and role play of a community job. "Painting" uses grasping skills and large arm movements.

(Social & Emotional Process, Creative Process, Physical Development Process)

What You Need To Make It

bleach bottle, washed well

needle & strong thread

thick elastic

scissors

plastic juice can

ice cream bucket

colored contact paper

wire hanger

2 or 3 large thread spools

pliers

adhesive tape

strip of foam material

waterproof glue

OR: any can or plastic tube, burlap, thin sponge, yarn or other thin absorbent material, strips of plastic and stapler, scratch awl or heated nail, etc.

How To Make It

① Cut the bleach bottle in the shape of a visor: first cut straight around just under the handle. Then cut a curved edge as shown. (Save the unused plastic for other toy projects!)

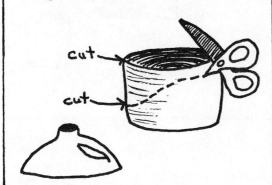

cut →
cut →

② Cut 8 small holes near the top of the visor: 2 each at the front, back and opposite sides as shown.

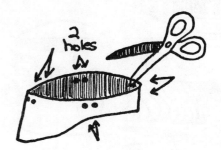

2 holes

③ Cut 2 strips of elastic long enough to go from the front to back, and from side to side.

④ Sew the ends of elastic to the inside of the visor through the holes.

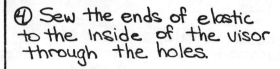
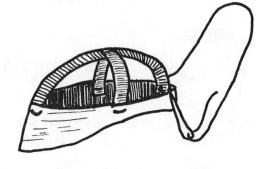

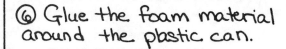

⑤ Cut out the words "paint" and "painter" from contact paper and put them on the bucket and the visor.

⑥ Glue the foam material around the plastic can.

WATER PROOF glue

⑦ Stretch out the wire hanger and "thread" it through the holes in the spools.

⑧ Put the hanger through the plastic can so the spools are _inside_ the can.

⑨ Bend the hanger to form a handle.

⑩ Cover the handle end with adhesive tape so the sharp ends of the hanger are covered well.

Scoop Catch

Age Group: Preschool, School Age

How To Use It:
Two children stand apart from each other, then toss and catch the ball back and forth using the scoops. Younger children may roll it back and forth with the scoops.

Foam or pompom ball can be used indoors, tennis ball outdoors.

What It Does:
Tossing and catching uses arm muscles, grasping skills, and eye-hand skills. Also encourages children to play together.
(Physical Development Process, Sensory & Perceptual Process, Social & Emotional Process)

Another Way To Make It:
Attach a pom pom ball to the handle of each scoop with yarn or string and child may try to swing it into the scoop.

What You Need To Make It

scissors   tennis ball

water

soap

2 bleach bottles, with or without caps

colored contact paper

OR: any soft ball, pom pom ball, colored material & glue, etc.

How To Make It

① Wash the bleach bottles well with soap and water.

② Carefully cut each bleach bottle to make a scoop. (Save the bottom for other toy projects!)

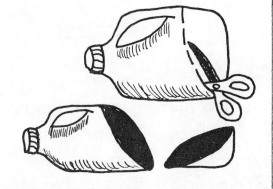

③ Cut out shapes from the contact paper.

④ Decorate the scoops with the shapes.

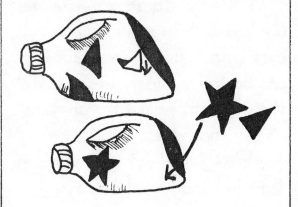

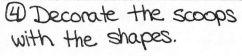
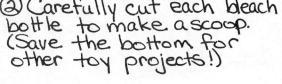

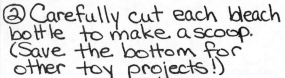

SANDWICH BAG PICTURE BOOK

AGE GROUP: Toddler, Preschool, School Age

HOW TO USE IT:

The pictures can be described or "read" by or to the child; encourage the child to invent stories to fit the pictures, or take turns describing them to each other.

Older children can make their own books, either drawing or cutting out their own pictures and having an older person write the story they narrate, or doing it all themselves.

Books need not have words in them to be enjoyed!

WHAT IT DOES:

The books encourage an interest in reading activities, and give practice "reading" from left to right, turning pages, etc. Describing pictures and storytelling encourage verbal expression and creativity. "Reading" with another person provides a way for the child to learn new words, concepts, and information about the world. It also helps to develop social and listening skills.

(Cognitive & Symbolic, Creative, Social & Emotional Processes)

What You Need To Make It:

4 to 8 plastic "ziplock" sandwich bags

 tagboard

old picture magazines OR paper and crayons or felt tip pens

thread & needle
(sewing machine is handy but not necessary)

 glue

How To Make It:

① Cut a piece of tagboard to fit inside each bag, equal in height and **¾" shorter** than the width of the bag. (Measure the bag with the open end on the left, as shown.)

¾"

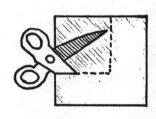

② Cut out pictures from magazines and glue them to **each** side of the tagboard pieces.

③ Slip each piece of tagboard into a plastic bag, with the open end of the bag at the left. Sew the open ends together securely with needle and thread.

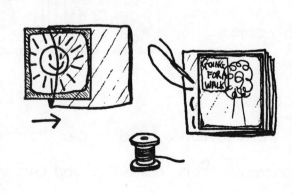

Book Ideas

—PEOPLE books   Pictures of each child with their names written underneath will encourage self-concept and name learning.

Make books with pictures of family and friends!

—FEELINGS books

—"THINGS THAT"... fly
talk
run
(or anything that's new or familiar!)

—COLORS books

—COUNTING books

—ETC.!

~Action Books are Fun!

Sew some of the book "pages" so the "ziplock" opening is at the top (instead of the sewn side).

All kinds of "things to do" can be inserted in these pockets:

How many square or rectangle designs can you make?

Balloon Puzzle

    puzzles

    matching games

    tricks

    lacing cards

    origami instructions (and paper to try them)

    or any active, fun activity you can invent!

RIDING HORSE

AGE GROUP: PRESCHOOL, SCHOOL AGE

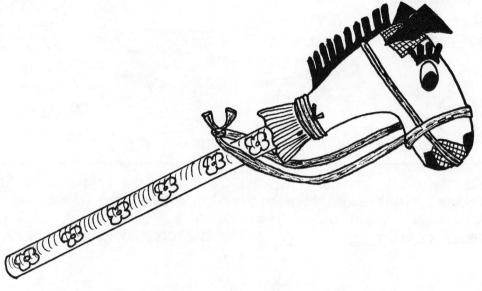

HOW TO USE IT:

The child straddles the dowel and "rides" the horse. This is an indoor or outdoor toy that can be used in all sorts of make-believe play.

Talk about horses, what they eat and do, and how they are alike and different from other animals!

WHAT IT DOES:

The horse encourages creative dramatic play, and walking and running skills.

It also encourages interest and learning about animals and their habits, and can help to foster respect for other living things.

(Creative, Physical Development, Cognitive & Symbolic Processes)

WHAT YOU NEED TO MAKE IT:

3' thick dowel OR broom-stick, or stiff cardboard tubes, fitted one into the other to make a long tube

8" x 40" strip of fabric OR vinyl

one old clean sock

2 carpet tacks

felt or fabric scraps

Polyester Fiber Fill

glue

5' ribbon OR string

OR old clean stockings

HOW TO MAKE IT:

① Fold the strip of material lengthwise, right sides together. Stitch a ½" seam along the 2 short edges only.

Right sides together

② Turn so the right side faces out. Place the dowel in between the fabric, and pad it all around with stuffing.

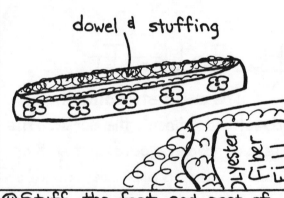

dowel & stuffing

Polyester Fiber Fill

③ Sew the remaining long seam closed.

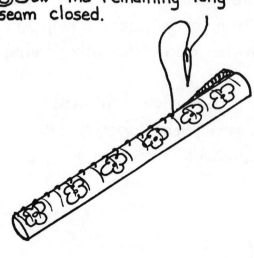

④ Stuff the foot and part of the leg of the sock until plump and full.

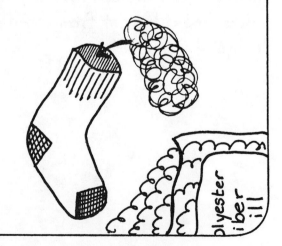

Polyester Fiber Fill

⑤ Push one end of the padded dowel into the sock.
Add more stuffing between the dowel and the sock.

⑥ Tie the sock securely to the stick with about 1' of ribbon.
Tack the sock to the dowel with carpet tacks.

⑦ Sew ribbon around the head and nose, and tie on reins.

⑧ Cut out mane, eyes, ears, nose and mouth pieces out of felt and fabric scraps.
Glue and sew them onto the sock securely.

BOARD GAME

AGE GROUP: School Age

HOW TO USE IT:

Two to four people play this game together. Each player has a button for a place marker. Players take turns spinning the color wheel. They match the color on the wheel to the colors on the spaces, and move along the path until they reach the end.

Preschoolers may not be too interested in the "rules" of the game, but often enjoy moving the pieces around the board. With all children, name the colors as you go; discuss the pictures and make up stories to go with them!

WHAT IT DOES:

This board game lets children practice their color matching skills. It encourages play with other children and promotes sharing, taking turns, etc.

Talking about the pictures promotes verbal expression and creativity. This encourages an interest in the <u>process</u> as well as the end result of the game.

(Cognitive & Symbolic, Social & Emotional Processes)

WHAT YOU NEED TO MAKE IT:

tagboard 15" x 15" (or any size)

tag-board 6"x6"

Clear contact paper

scissors

paper fastener

masking tape

plastic drinking straw OR tongue depressor

4 buttons of different colors or shapes

4 felt tip markers of different colors

HOW TO MAKE IT:

① Draw a path on the tagboard; divide it into 1" squares and color in the squares with the 4 colors of markers. Draw some "slides" too.

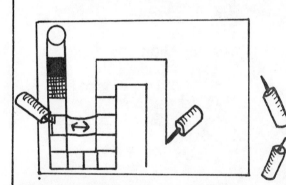

② Draw pictures along the path that have a theme or tell a story. (for example, writing a letter to a friend)

③ Draw a circle on the smaller piece of tagboard and divide it into four parts. Color each part a different color to match the board spaces.

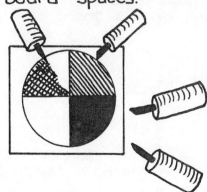

④ Cover both pieces of tagboard with clear contact paper.

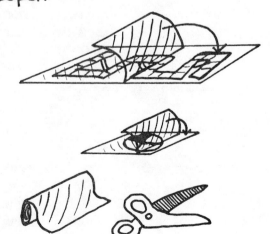

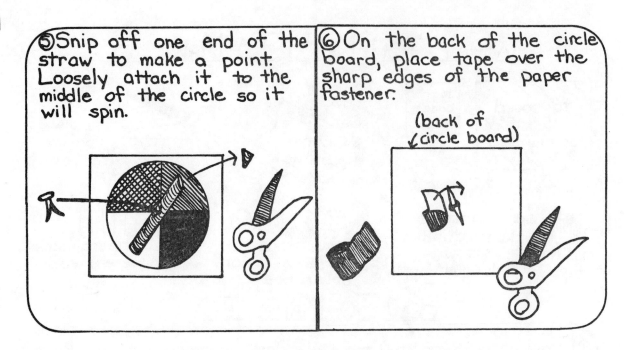

⑤ Snip off one end of the straw to make a point. Loosely attach it to the middle of the circle so it will spin.

⑥ On the back of the circle board, place tape over the sharp edges of the paper fastener.

(back of circle board)

<u>VARIATIONS</u> are endless...

Make <u>BOARDS</u> from:

cardboard
stiff paper
old game boards
  (cover with contact paper)
pieces of shower curtain
  or plastic
linoleum pieces
ETC.

Use as <u>PLACE MARKERS</u>:

bottle caps
jar lids
paper clips
dried beans
cardboard shapes
thread spools
pipe cleaner figures
washers
ETC.

<u>SPINNER ALTERNATIVES</u>:

throwing dice
drawing numbered discs of any kind
drawing cards with instructions on them
drawing objects from a sock to
  match something on the board
ETC.

The <u>PATH</u> can be:

drawn
painted
pictures cut from magazines or comics
rug pieces or colored or textured material
dime store stickers
ETC.

Board <u>TASKS</u>:

    match numbers
    number sums
    number multiples
    rhyming words
    word endings
    word beginnings
    match textures
    match cities with states
    match capital and small letters
    match shapes
    ETC.

Board <u>THEMES</u> can be used to introduce or explain new or "mysterious" events, processes or ideas. They can help prepare or remind children of upcoming (or recent) field trips.
Some examples are:
    following food products from the farm to the store to the table
    following cars from raw materials at the factory through the assembly line to home
    going to the hospital
    going on a trip
    ETC.

Let your children draw their own boards too!

Store the boards and pieces in a box.

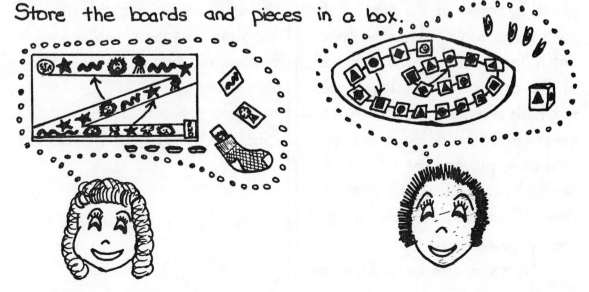

DOMINOES

AGE GROUP: PRESCHOOL, SCHOOL AGE

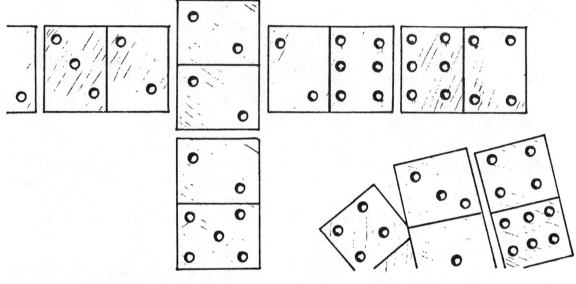

HOW TO USE IT:

This is a fun game for two or more people to play together.

Let each person draw 4-6 dominoes from the envelope in which they are stored. To begin, place 1 domino in the center; then take turns adding dominoes that match the number on the free side of the domino. If a player does not have a match, draw from the envelope until a match comes up. When one player uses up all of her or his dominoes, the game is done. Count how many dominoes are in your chain!

This can also be a 1-person game!

WHAT IT DOES:

The game task helps to develop matching skills and an understanding of number concepts.

Playing with other children encourages sharing, learning to take turns, and finding out how much fun other people can be!

(Cognitive & Symbolic, Social & Emotional Processes)

WHAT YOU NEED TO MAKE IT:

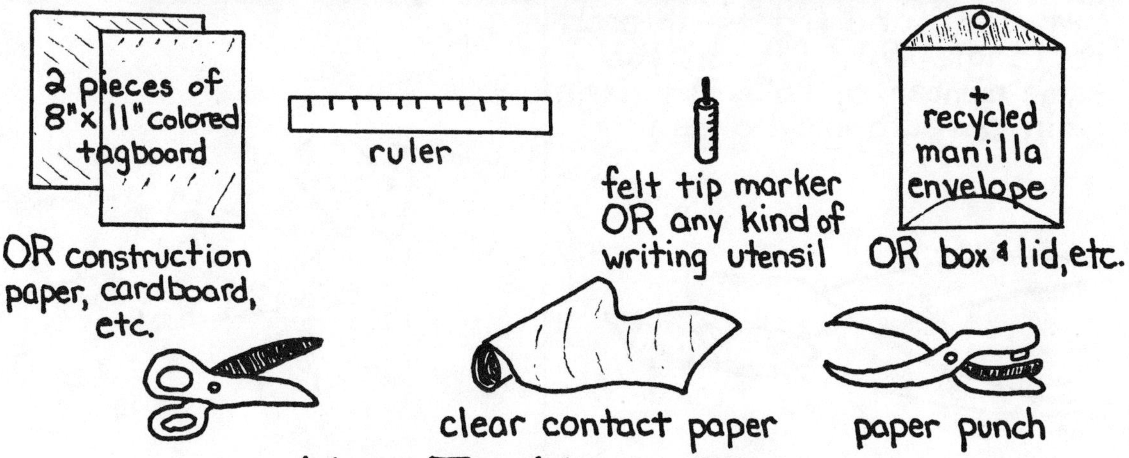

2 pieces of 8"x 11" colored tagboard

OR construction paper, cardboard, etc.

ruler

felt tip marker OR any kind of writing utensil

recycled manilla envelope

OR box & lid, etc.

clear contact paper

paper punch

HOW TO MAKE IT:

① With a marker, draw 12 rectangles on each piece of tagboard, roughly 2" x 3⅔" in size.

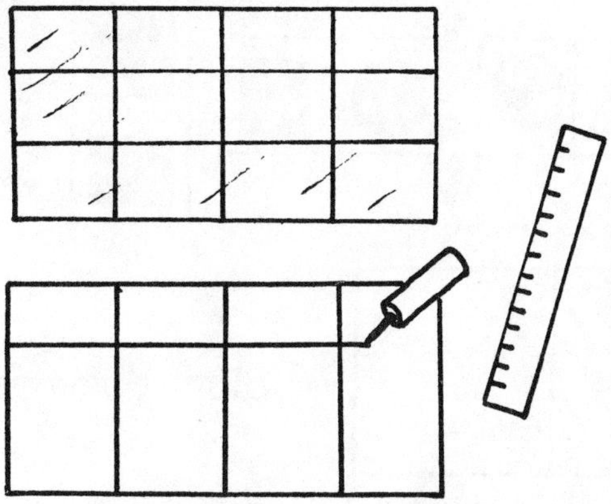

② Draw a line through the middle of each rectangle from one long side to the other.

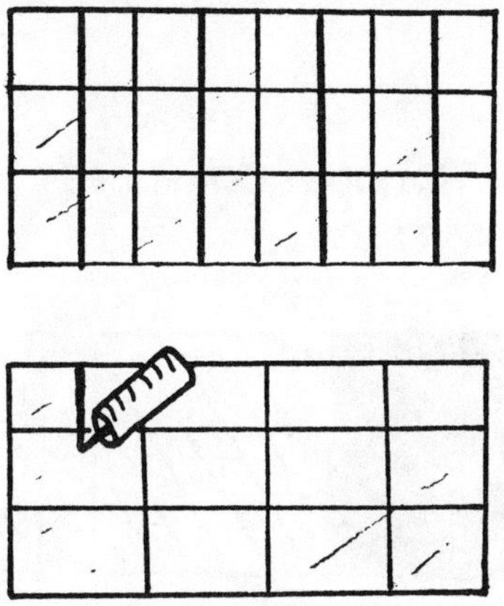

③ Cover BOTH sides of the tagboard with contact paper.

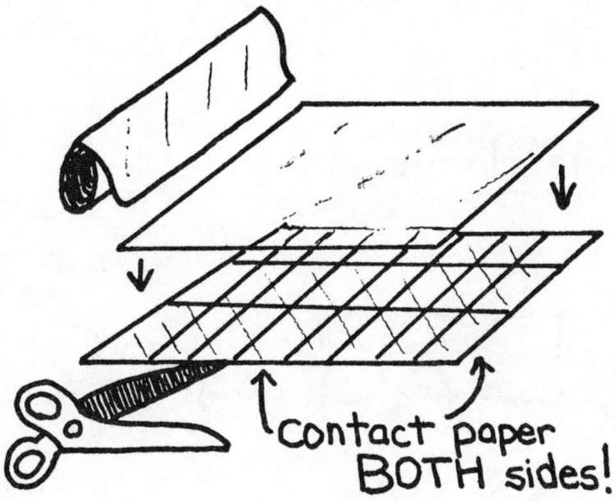

Contact paper BOTH sides!

④ Cut out the rectangles you drew in step ①.

⑤In random order, punch between 1 and 6 dots in each rectangle half. (Punch the same number of holes -1 through 6-in **8** rectangle halves.)

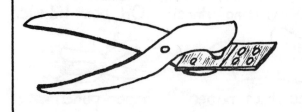

⑥Store in the manilla envelope.

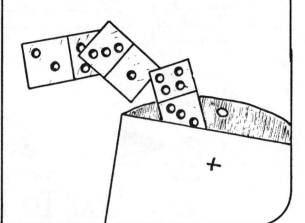

VARIATIONS

Shape dominoes

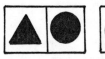

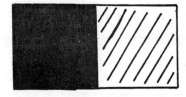 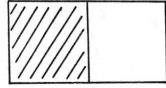

Color dominoes

Dime store sticker dominoes

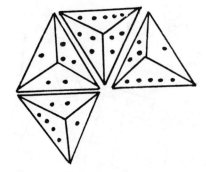

Triangle dominoes

BIG dominoes

little dominoes

etc. etc. etc. etc.

MATCHING PUZZLES

AGE GROUP: PRESCHOOL, SCHOOL AGE

TAGBOARD

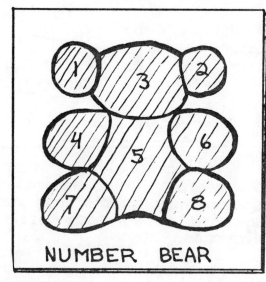

NUMBER BEAR

HOW TO USE IT:

The child matches the pieces to the puzzle board by number and shape.

WHAT IT DOES:

Puzzles encourage problem-solving and learning how parts fit together. They also develop eye-hand and finger coordination skills.

The tasks of the matching puzzle develop matching and counting skills too!

(Creative, Cognitive & Symbolic, Physical Development, Sensory & Perceptual Processes)

WHAT YOU NEED TO MAKE IT:

8"x11" colored tagboard

OR cardboard & construction paper

8"x11" cardboard

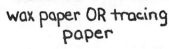
wax paper OR tracing paper

10¢
dime
OR coding dots, dime store stickers, paper & paper punch

glue

felt tip marker

clear contact paper

HOW TO MAKE IT:

① Trace the pattern of the bear (see next page) onto wax paper. Cut out the wax paper pattern along the <u>outer</u> edge, and trace it onto the tagboard.

wax paper pattern

② Outline the puzzle pieces. Using the dime, trace and color in the right number of dots for each puzzle piece.

③ Cover the tagboard with clear contact paper.

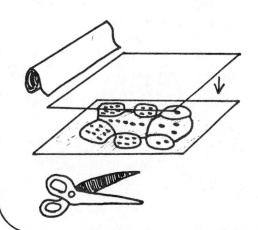

④ Cut out the 8 puzzle pieces, being careful <u>not to cut into</u> the <u>outer background area</u>.

outer background area

TRACE ALL THE LINES.

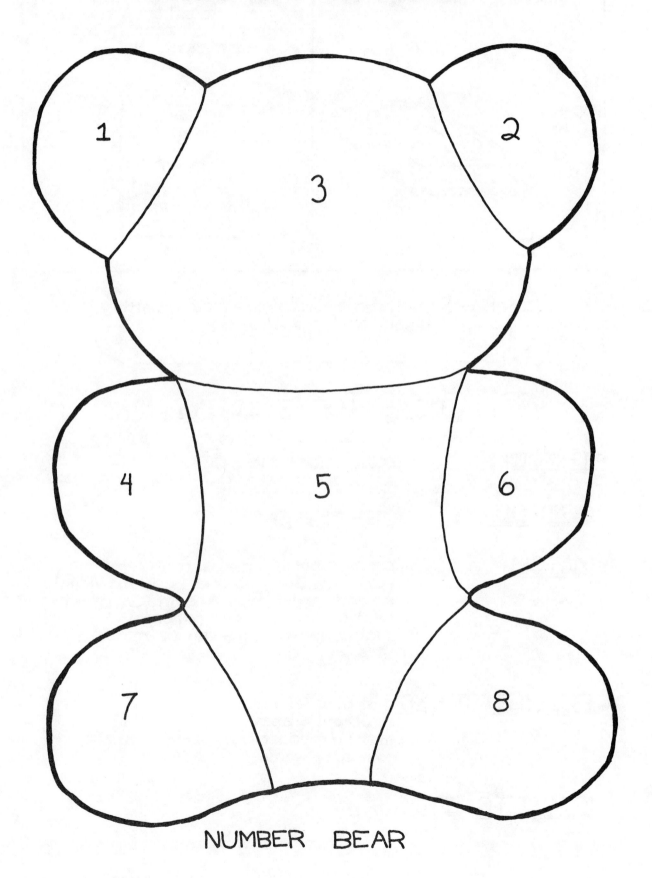

NUMBER BEAR

⑤Glue the background section of tagboard to the cardboard.

⑥Trace the puzzle shapes on the cardboard to show how they fit together. Write the number that corresponds with each dot.

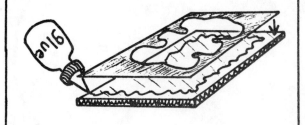

✱Store the puzzle in a recycled manilla envelope or box and lid!

IDEAS IDEAS IDEAS

TRACE: coloring book pictures

CUT OUT: magazine pictures

MATCH: contact paper designs from repeating
                 patterns: Cut out and back individual
                 objects and match them to an intact
                 section of contact paper.
                 Wallpaper designs can be matched
                 this way too.

PUZZLE TASKS: matching letters
                 matching shapes
                 matching upper and lower case letters
                 matching words

ETC. ETC. ETC.

PICTURE MATCHING BOARD

AGE GROUP: PRESCHOOL, SCHOOL AGE

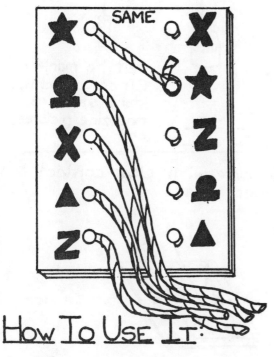

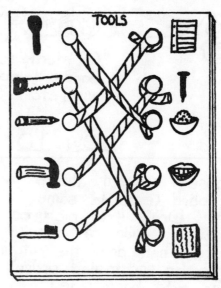

HOW TO USE IT:

The child matches pictures on the left side of the board with pictures on the right side by wrapping a piece of yarn around the paper fastener next to the matching picture.

Each card can have a different task: pictures can go together using concepts such as "same", "opposite", or other sorting categories like food, clothes, colors, etc. Discuss these concepts with the child. Larger boards with more items are challenging for schoolagers.

WHAT IT DOES:

The board task encourages an understanding of a number of basic concepts. It also helps to develop hand and finger coordination.

(Cognitive & Symbolic, Physical Development Processes)

WHAT YOU NEED TO MAKE IT:

2 - 8"x11" pieces of tagboard (or any size)

clear contact paper

8-12 paper fasteners

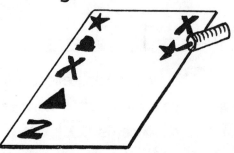
(scissors)

YARN
OR sturdy rubber bands, telephone wire, etc.

glue

felt tip marker OR crayons, dime store stickers, magazine pictures, etc.

HOW TO MAKE IT:

① Choose a concept theme for your board (example: same shapes.) Draw 4-6 pictures on the left side of one tagboard. Then draw the matching pictures (in scrambled order) on the right hand side.

② Cover with clear contact paper.

③ Attach a paper fastener next to each shape. Wrap a piece of yarn to each fastener on the left.

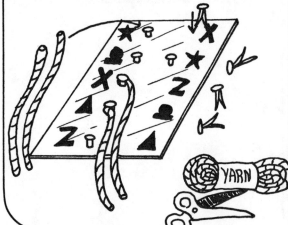
YARN

④ Glue the second piece of tagboard to the back side of the first piece so the paper fastener ends are covered.

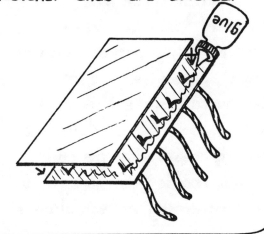
glue

SPOOL SNAKE

AGE GROUP: TODDLER, PRESCHOOL

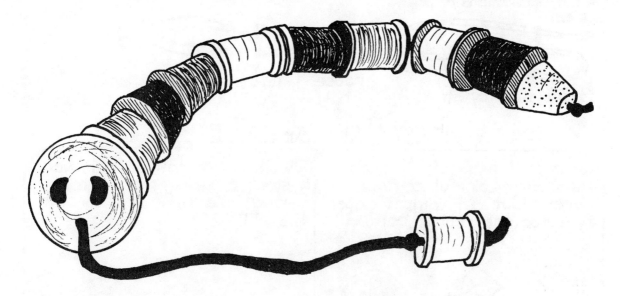

HOW TO USE IT:

The snake is pulled by the string.

It can be used in fantasy play: what adventures can you and your child invent? The snake can also be used in discussions about reptiles.

WHAT IT DOES:

The spool snake encourages toddlers to practice their new skills in walking; it also encourages them to turn around and walk backwards to watch the cause-and-effect relationship of pulling the string and movement.

The spool snake promotes fantasy play, and learning about animals too.

(Physical Development, Cognitive & Symbolic, Creative Processes)

WHAT YOU NEED TO MAKE IT:

8-12 wooden or styrofoam thread spools (NOT plastic) OR cut-up sections of plastic bottles

contact paper

OR paint (for wooden spools)

cork

3-3½ ft. sturdy string

rubber ball

large nail

pliers OR potholder

stove top

HOW TO MAKE IT:

① Cover the middle of each spool with colorful contact paper. Cut out contact paper eyes for the rubber ball.

② With a hot nail (heat it over a stove burner), melt a hole through the cork and through the ball.

hole

③ Tie a knot in one end of the string. Thread through the other end: the cork, all BUT 1 spool, and the ball.

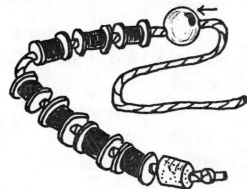

④ At the other end of the string, tie a knot about 3" from the end. Slip on the last spool, and tie another knot. This makes a handle.

Bongo Drum

Age Group: Infants, Toddlers, Preschool, School Age

How To Use It:

Child beats on drum to singing, other instruments, records, or his or her inner rhythms!

What It Does:

Helps music and rhythm expression, encourages listening skills and active movement.

(Creative Process, Sensory & Perceptual Process, Physical Development Process)

What You Need To Make It

 coffee can

 string

 old inner tube

 crayons

 glue

 paper

scissors

wooden spoon or dowel

<u>OR</u>: any cardboard or metal can, contact paper, etc.

How To Make It

① Cut a piece of paper to fit the outside of the can.

② Draw a design on the paper with crayons.

③ Glue the paper to the can.

④ Cut a circle out of the inner tube · a few inches bigger than the rim of the can.

⑤ Put the circle on the __open__ end of the can and wrap string around to hold it tight. Tie a knot.

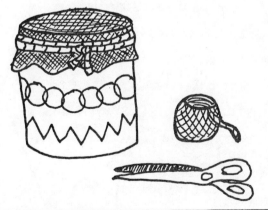

⑥ Check the wooden spoon or dowel to make sure it is "kid-proof": __smooth__ and __without__ __sharp__ or __splintery__ __edges__.

Nesting Cans

Age Group: Toddlers, Preschool

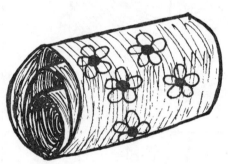

How To Use It:
Child may practice putting the cans inside one another and taking them out. When turned over, they can be stacked to make towers. Younger children may roll them back and forth. Adult may discuss "small, smaller, big, biggest", etc. with older children.

What It Does:
Helps understanding of size differences and may teach word concepts. Encourages creative building play. Rolling back and forth develops pushing skills.
(Cognitive & Symbolic Process, Creative Process, Physical Development Process)

Other Ways To Use It:
The words "biggest", "big", "small", "smallest" could be written on the cans for school age children and used in measuring experiments.

What You Need To Make It

5-6 cans of increasing size - open at one end

can opener

Scissors

colorful contact paper

OR: any boxes or tubes of increasing size, magazine pictures and clear contact paper, etc.

How To Make It

① Go around the rim of each clean can several times with the can opener to make sure there are no sharp edges.

② Cut contact paper one inch **longer** than each can. Cover each can with the contact paper, folding the extra over the rim. Put the cans inside each other.

Pom Pom Grasp & Pull Toy

Age Group: Infants, Toddlers

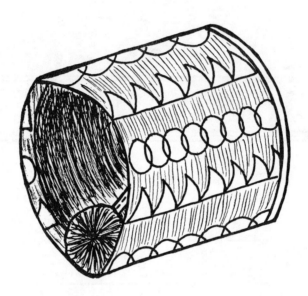

How To Use It:
Child grasps the pom pom inside the can and pulls it towards him or herself; elastic attached to the pom pom and lid makes the pom pom pop back into the can when the child lets go of it.

What It Does:
Bright colors attract the child to the toy; encourages grasping and pulling skills.

(Physical Development Process, Sensory & Perceptual Process)

What You Need To Make It

coffee can
& lid

thick elastic

yarn

needle
& thread

scissors

can opener

piece of cardboard
about 5"x5"

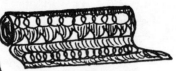
colorful contact paper

OR: any metal can and plastic lid, magazine pictures
and clear contact paper, etc.

How To Make It

① Take off the metal ends of the can. Go around the rims several times to make sure they are smooth.

both ends

② Cover the can with contact paper, making the contact paper about 1 inch longer at each end. Fold this extra over into the inside of the can.

③ Cut a piece of elastic the same length as the can.

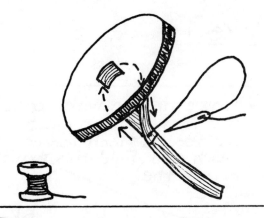

④ Cut 2 slits in the middle of the plastic lid, large enough for the elastic to go through.

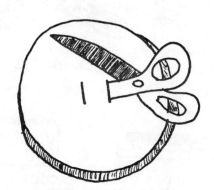

⑤ From the inside of the lid, lace one end of the elastic through the slits, and sew it securely as shown.

⑥ Make a yarn pom pom (as shown on the next page).

⑦ Sew the other end of the elastic to the pom pom.

⑧ Put the lid on the can so the pom pom and elastic are inside.

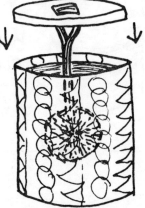

How To Make A Yarn Ball or "Pom-Pom"

① Wind any kind of yarn loosely around a 5" wide piece of cardboard - about 50 times. (Changing the width of the cardboard makes the ball bigger or smaller.)

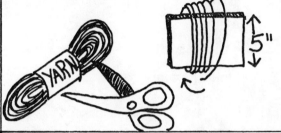

② With a differently colored piece of yarn, tie the wound yarn together on one side of the cardboard.

Then push the yarn off the cardboard.

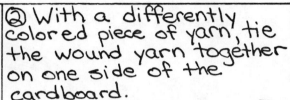

③ Tie the yarn together in the middle with another piece of yarn as shown.

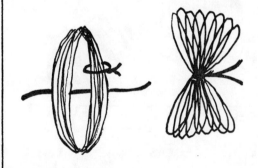

④ Cut the loops.

⑤ Repeat steps ① - ④ above about 3 or 4 times and tie all of these balls together to make 1 large ball.

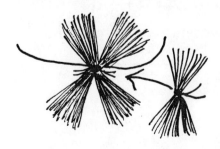

⑥ To prevent curious children from pulling out the yarn strands, the balls may be put in old nylon stockings and tied with string.

Self-Help Sally (or Sam)

Age Group: Preschool, (early) School Age

How To Use It:
Child practices lacing and tying doll's shoes, buttoning and unbuttoning coat, combing and braiding or ponytailing yarn hair.
Younger children may need help and praise from an older person.

What It Does:
Child learns and practices how to dress him or herself. Also helps teach body parts.

(Social & Emotional Development Process)

What You Need To Make It

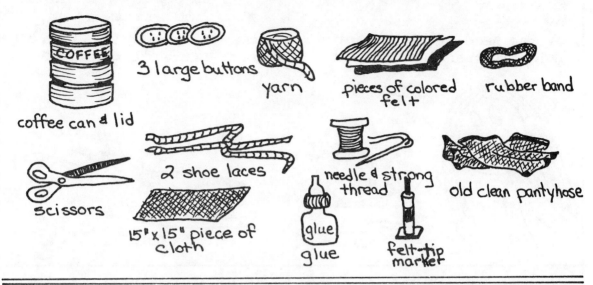

coffee can & lid

3 large buttons

yarn

pieces of colored felt

rubber band

scissors

2 shoe laces

15"x15" piece of cloth

needle & strong thread

glue

felt-tip marker

old clean pantyhose

<u>OR</u>: any large can & lid, vinyl or heavy material or cardboard or old socks, yarn or string, strips of newspaper or clean rags. or lots of lint from a clothes dryer, hankerchief, etc.

How To Make It

① Put the pantyhose in the middle of the 15"x15" piece of material. Tie it together with a rubber band to make a roundish head.

② Draw eyes, nose and mouth with the felt-tip marker. (Press lightly so the marks do not spread out.)

158

③ Cut equal lengths of yarn, fold them in half, and sew the folded part to the top of the head securely for hair, all the way around.

④ Cut 3 small crossing slits in the center of the lid.
Then, with the tip of the scissors, punch 10-12 small holes near the center of the lid.

slits

holes

⑤ Push the bottom end of the head through the slits so just the head shows on top.

⑥ Turn the head and lid over. Sew through the leftover cloth and the holes in the lid so the head stays firmly on.

⑦ Cut enough felt to go around the coffee can and overlap about 2 inches for a coat.

+2"

⑧ Cut out 2 arms and 2 legs of felt. Make them simple!

legs

arms

⑨ Wrap the coat around the can. Cut 2 slits in the felt, just big enough for the arms, near the top on either side.

slits in felt

⑩ Push the ends of the arms through the slits. Sew securely to the coat on the underside.

⑪ Put on the lid. Glue the back half of the coat to the can, <u>leaving the front half unglued</u>.

glue

⑫ Sew 3 buttons on the left side of the coat.

⑬ Cut out a felt heart and glue it to the right side of the can.

glue

⑭ Cut buttonholes so the coat can be buttoned around the can.

160

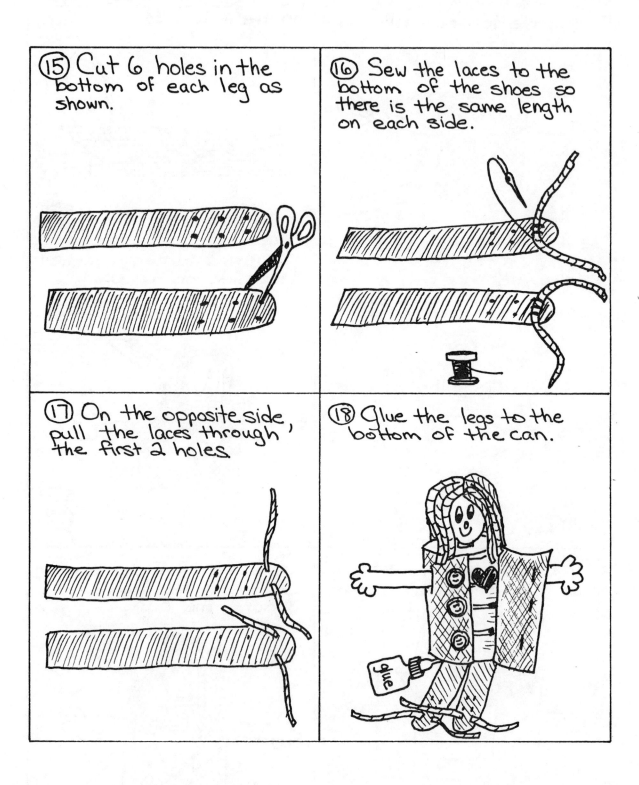

(15) Cut 6 holes in the bottom of each leg as shown.

(16) Sew the laces to the bottom of the shoes so there is the same length on each side.

(17) On the opposite side, pull the laces through the first 2 holes.

(18) Glue the legs to the bottom of the can.

Shape Sorting Can

Age Group: Toddlers, Preschool

How To Use It:

Show the child how objects fit into differently shaped holes in the top of the can, naming each shape as you demonstrate with a few objects. Child may experiment to discover which objects fit into which holes, then opening the can and dumping them back out. (All objects need not fit exactly)

What It Does:

Helps child become aware of shapes and how objects are alike or different by shape. Also gives child practice using his or her hands.

(Cognitive & Symbolic Process, Physical Development Process)

<u>What</u> <u>You</u> <u>Need</u> <u>To</u> <u>Make</u> <u>It</u>

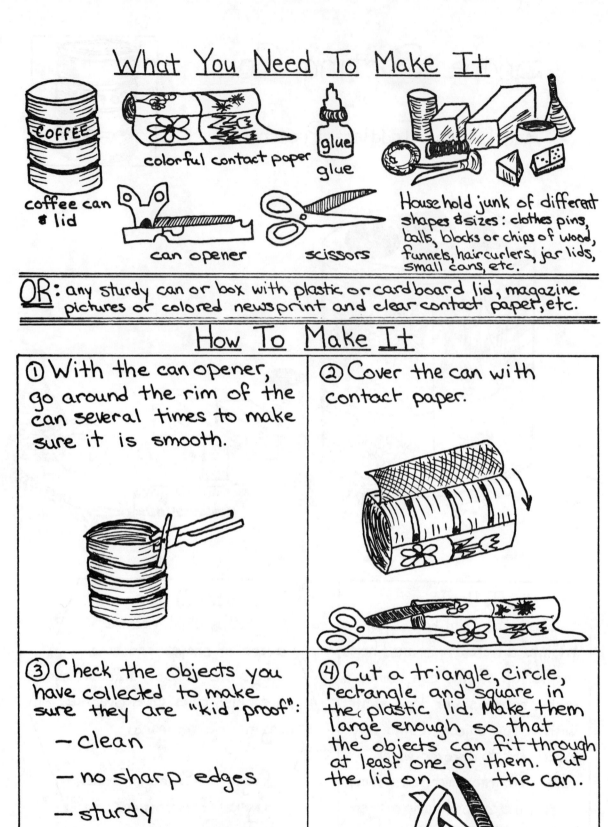

coffee can & lid

colorful contact paper

glue

can opener

scissors

Household junk of different shapes & sizes: clothes pins, balls, blocks or chips of wood, funnels, haircurlers, jar lids, small cans, etc.

<u>OR</u>: any sturdy can or box with plastic or cardboard lid, magazine pictures or colored newsprint and clear contact paper, etc.

<u>How</u> <u>To</u> <u>Make</u> <u>It</u>

① With the can opener, go around the rim of the can several times to make sure it is smooth.

② Cover the can with contact paper.

③ Check the objects you have collected to make sure they are "kid-proof":

- clean

- no sharp edges

- sturdy

- too large to be swallowed.

④ Cut a triangle, circle, rectangle and square in the plastic lid. Make them large enough so that the objects can fit through at least one of them. Put the lid on the can.

Tin Can Musical Rolling Pin

Age Group: Infants, Toddlers.

<u>How To Use It</u>:

   Infants may roll it back and forth;

   crawlers may push it along in front of themselves;

   and toddlers may pull it on a string.

<u>What It Does</u>:

   Bright colors attract the child to the toy; the music and rattles encourage listening skills; the rolling of the toy encourages pushing and grasping skills, or pulling and walking skills. (Sensory & Perceptual Process, Physical Development Process)

What You Need To Make It

coffee can   12 - 18" sturdy dowel   pencil   sandpaper

2 plastic lids to fit the can   string   mineral oil   clean rag

can opener   scissors   bells and/or small jar lids

colorful contact paper

OR: shortening or other metal can, broom handle or stiff tubing, colored newsprint or magazine pictures and clear contact paper, anything that rattles

How To Make It

① Take off the metal ends of the coffee can. Go around the rims several times with a can opener to make sure they are smooth.

both ends

② Tie together the bells with string so they are too big to be swallowed. Put the small jar lids, bells, and other noise makers inside the can.

③ With a pencil trace around the dowel in the middle of each plastic lid. Cut a ✳ in the middle of each circle.

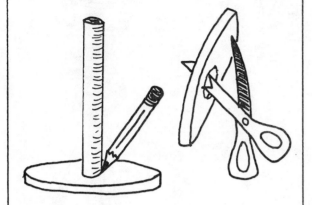

④ Put the lids on the can.

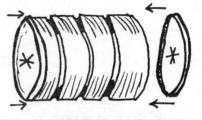

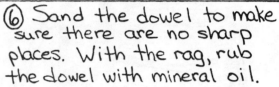

⑤ Cover the can with contact paper.

⑥ Sand the dowel to make sure there are no sharp places. With the rag, rub the dowel with mineral oil.

⑦ Push the dowel through the star-shaped cuts in the lids so there is a handle at both ends.

Tin Can Stilts

Age Group: Preschool, School Age

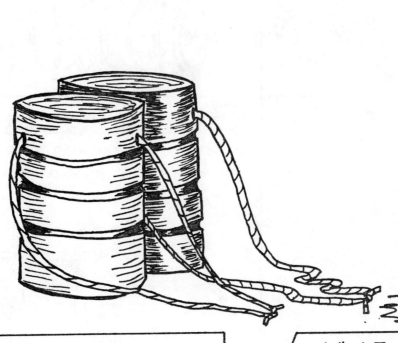

<u>How To Use It</u>:
Child puts one foot on each can and holds one rope in each hand. By pulling up on one rope at a time, the child can walk with the stilts on flat ground.

<u>What It Does</u>:
Helps the child learn and practice balance and coordination skills.

(Physical Development Process)

What You Need To Make It

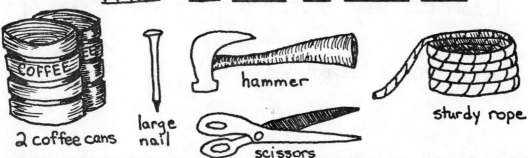

2 coffee cans   large nail   hammer   scissors   sturdy rope

OR: large juice cans with puncture holes in the tops, etc.

How To Make It

① Make 2 holes on opposite sides of each can (1 to 2 inches from the bottom) with the nail and hammer. Make sure the outside of each hole is not sharp.

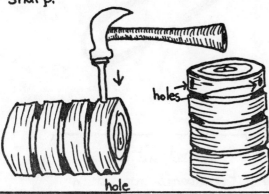

holes

hole

② Cut 2 pieces of rope, each twice the length from the child's feet to waist.

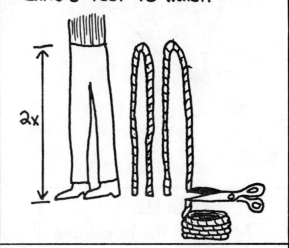

2x

③ Push one end of the rope through the holes in the cans.

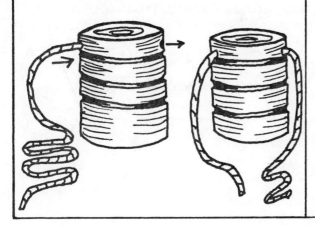

④ Tie the ends securely together.

Butterfly Net

Age Group: School Age

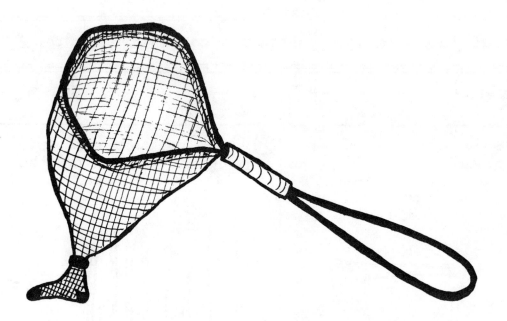

How To Use It:

By holding the handle and running, the child may catch flying insects. Insect could then be placed in a "Bug keeper" for a short time. Older children could be encouraged to identify and read about the insect.

What It Does:

Encourages interest in insects, and can help fear of them. Helps develop an understanding of other living things. May encourage science reading.

(Cognitive & Symbolic Process, Social & Emotional Process)

What You Need To Make It

2 wire hangers

adhesive tape

old clean stocking

needle & thread

rubber band

pliers

6" stiff piece of hose

<u>OR</u>: cheesecloth or netting, stapler, electrical tape, thread spools or stiff tubing, etc.

How To Make It

① Bend one hanger into a diamond shape and straighten out the handle.

Stretch out the second hanger so it is almost straight. Wrap the handles of the 2 hangers together

② Tape the ends so there are no sharp points.

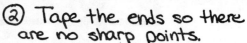

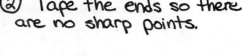

③ Push the stiff piece of hose over the second hanger until it covers the taped part as shown.

If necessary, tape it in place.

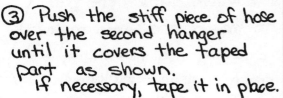

④ Stretch the top of the stocking around the diamond shaped hanger and sew it on. Put a rubber band near the feet of the stocking.

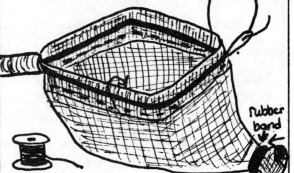

rubber band

Crib Mobile

Age Group: Infants

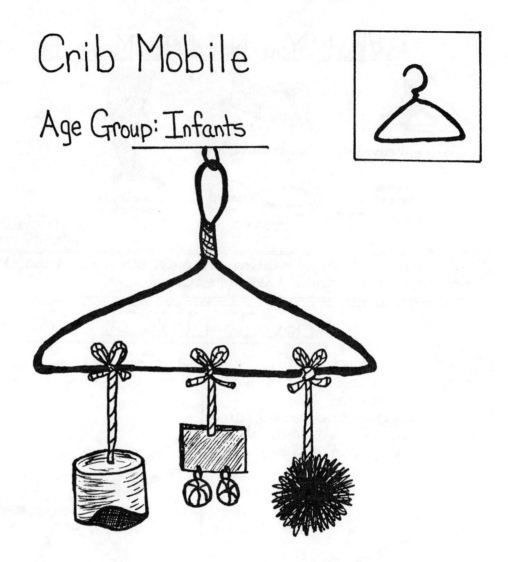

How To Use It:
Hang the mobile <u>securely</u> <u>above</u> the crib (<u>not</u> <u>in</u> it) so the objects are about 12" from the infant's eyes. The objects will move in a breeze. Or, an adult may move the hanger back and forth in an arch so the infant will follow it with his or her eyes.

What It Does:
Bright colors and movement attract the baby to the objects, encouraging focusing, eye movements, and general visual development. (Sensory & Perceptual Process)

<u>New</u> <u>Objects</u> (any colorful, safe household material) may be substituted once a week or so to give the baby something new to watch. Changing only one or two objects at a time is a good idea.

What You Need To Make It

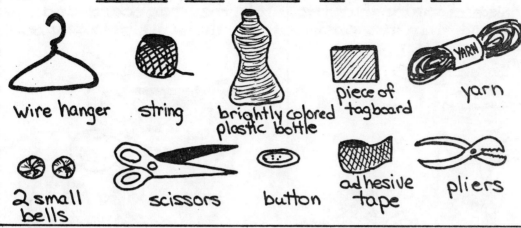

wire hanger   string   brightly colored plastic bottle   piece of tagboard   yarn

2 small bells   scissors   button   adhesive tape   pliers

OR: wide band elastic, any brightly colored. lightweight objects, thread spool, etc.

How To Make It

① Cut the plastic bottle in half.

② Cut a small hole in the bottom of the bottle.

172

③ Tie a knot at one end of a 6"-10" piece of string. Put the button and then the plastic bottle on the string as shown.

④ Cut 2 holes in one side of the tagboard and tie the 2 bells loosely on.

⑤ Cut a hole in the middle of the opposite side of the cardboard. Tie one end of a 4-8" string to it.

⑥ Make a pompom (see directions in "Pom Pom Grasp and Pull Toy"). Tie one end of a 6-10" piece of string to the pom pom.

⑦ Tie the free ends of the strings securely to the hanger.

⑧ With pliers bend the hook of the hanger over into a loop. Cover with tape so it is not sharp.

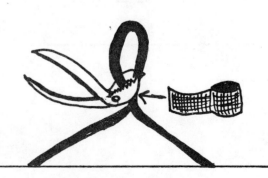

Paddle Ball

Age Group: Preschool, School Age

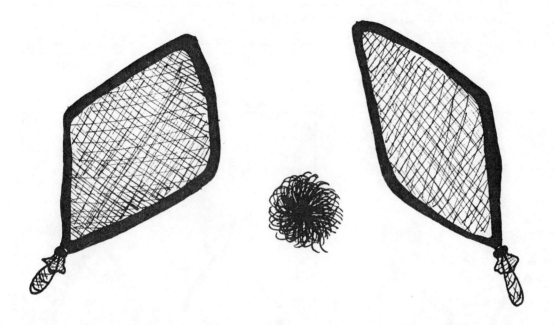

How To Use It:
Two children hit the fuzz ball back and forth with the paddles. A badminton birdie or foam ball may be used instead of a fuzz ball (or with older children, a balloon). Counting games may be played while hitting the ball.

What It Does:
Encourages play with other children. Helps eye-hand skills. May help understanding of number concepts.

(Social & Emotional Process, Sensory & Perceptual Process, Cognitive & Symbolic Process)

What You Need To Make It

2 wire hangers

1 pr. old clean stockings

adhesive tape

scissors

pliers

2 rubber bands

yarn

OR: badmitton birdie, foam ball, etc.

How To Make It

① Bend the hangers into a roundish or diamond shape. Bend in the handle.

② Cover the handle with adhesive tape so there are no sharp edges

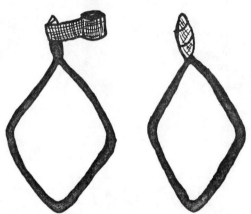

③ Slip a stocking over each hanger and tightly wrap a rubber band around the handles.

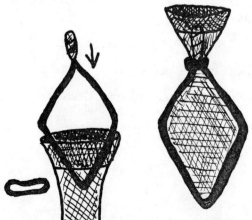

④ Cut off the extra stocking around the handle. Make a fuzz ball. (See directions with "Pom Pom Grasp & Pull Toy).

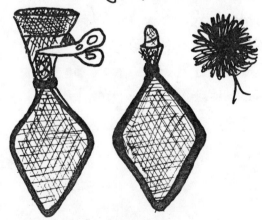

Pulley Toy

Age Group: Preschool, School Age

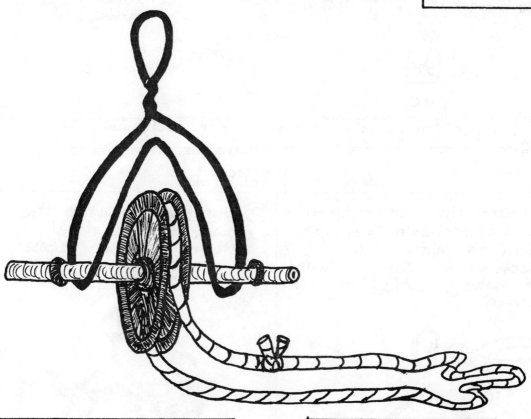

How To Use It:

Hanger can be hung on a chair, a curtain rod, clothes line, or tree limb. Pulley may go either at an angle upwards, or horizontally (from 1 play space to another.) Child may attach objects to the rope and send them to another child via pulley. May be used in building play and science games.

What It Does:

Helps child understand how simple machines work. Encourages role play of community jobs and dramatic play.

(Cognitive & Symbolic Process, Social & Emotional Process, Creative Process)

A Good "Carrier" to attach to the pulley rope may be made by making a hole in 1 side of a plastic bucket and tying 1 end of a rope to it. The contents can be then "dumped"

↑ pulley rope

176

What You Need To Make It

wire hanger

empty metal adhesive tape reel

½" diameter dowel

2 rubber bands

rope

glue

pliers

OR: Super 8 movie film reel, or other reel, yarn, tape, etc.

How To Make It

① Bend the hanger up into an upside down "V shape. With the pliers, bend the hook of the hanger inward to make a closed loop as shown.

② Slip the reel onto the dowel. Rest the dowel between the two "arms" of the hanger.

③ Put a rubber band on each end of the dowel near the hanger Glue them. (This keeps the dowel from slipping off of the hanger.)

rubber band

④ Tie a long rope around the reel as shown.

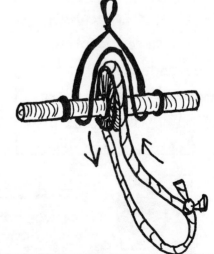

NOTES

Toys Grouped According To Age Guidelines

Infant:

Bongo Drum
Carpet Puzzles
Cause & Effect Match Board
Crawl-Over Box
Crib Mobile
Easy Grasp Ball
Finger Puppets
Fish Bowl Shaker Bottle
Foam Block Push Through
Hanging Mobiles
Lid Puppet
Milk Carton Blocks
Pom Pom Grasp & Pull Toy
Pop Up Puppet
Reversible Color & Design Sign
Rhythm Shakers
Stuffed Kick Toy
Texture Ball
Tin Can Musical Rolling Pin

Toddler:

Baker's Hat & Rolling Pin
Bongo Drum
Box Camera
Carpet Puzzles
Cause & Effect Match Board
Clothespin Matching Game
Easy Grasp Ball
Finger Puppets
Fish Bowl Shaker Bottle
Foam Block Push Through
Lid Puppet
Milk Carton Blocks
Musical Roller Pull Toy
Nesting Cans
Painter's Visor, Pail & Roller
Picture Puzzles
Pom Pom Grasp & Pull Toy
Pop Up Puppet
Rhythm Shakers
Riding Horse
Sandwich Bag Picture Book
Shape Sorting Can
Sliding Egg
Spool Snake
Styrofoam Bubble Boat
Texture Ball
Tin Can Musical Rolling Pin
Wagon

PRESCHOOL:

Back Pack & Sit-Upon
Baker's Hat & Rolling Pin
Binoculars
Bongo Drum
Box Camera
Carpet Puzzles
Clothespin Matching Game
Colored Button Sort
Dominoes
Fabric Matching Game
Face Masks
Feel & Tell Box
Felt Board
Finger Puppets
Fish Bowl Shaker Bottle
Foam Block Push Through
Following Footsteps Game
Kazoo
Lid Matching Puzzles
Lid Puppet
Limber Jenny or Joe
Mail Carrier's Cap & Bag
Mail Sorting Game
Matching Puzzles
Milk Carton Blocks
Milking Cow
Musical Roller Pull Toy
Nesting Cans

Paddle Ball
Painter's Visor, Pail & Roller
Picture Matching Board
Picture Puzzles
Plastic Lacing Cards
Pop Up Puppet
Pulley Toy
Rhythm Shakers
Riding Horse
Ring Catch
Sandwich Bag Picture Book
Scoop Catch
Self Help Sally or Sam
Shape Sorting Can
Sliding Egg
Spool Snake
Styrofoam Bubble Boat
Tin Can Stilts
Wagon

SCHOOL AGE:

Back Pack & Sit-Upon
Baker's Hat & Rolling Pin
Binoculars
Board Game
Bongo Drum
Box Camera
Bug Keeper
Butterfly Net
Clothespin Matching Game
Colored Button Sort
Dominoes
Fabric Matching Game
Face Masks
Feel & Tell Box
Felt Board
Finger Puppets
Following Footsteps Game
Kazoo
Lid Matching Puzzles
Lid Puppet
Limber Jenny or Joe
Mail Carrier's Cap & Bag
Mail Sorting Game
Matching Puzzles
Milk Carton Blocks
Milking Cow
Paddle Ball
Painter's Visor, Pail & Roller

Picture Matching Board
Picture Puzzles
Plastic Lacing Cards
Pop Up Puppet
Pulley Toy
Rhythm Shakers
Riding Horse
Ring Catch
Sandwich Bag Picture Book
Scoop Catch
Self Help Sally or Sam
Sliding Egg
Styrofoam Bubble Boat
Tin Can Stilts
Wagon

OTHER REDLEAF PRESS PUBLICATIONS

Basic Guide to Family Day Care Record Keeping — Clear instructions on keeping necessary family day care business records.

Business Receipt Book — Receipts specifically for family child care payments improve your record keeping; 50 sets per book.

Calendar-Keeper — Activities, family day care record keeping, recipes and more. Updated annually. Most popular publication in the field.

Child Care Resource & Referral Counselors & Trainers Manual — Both a ready reference for the busy phone counselor and a training guide for resource and referral agencies.

The Dynamic Infant — Combines an overview of child development with innovative movement and sensory experiences for infants and toddlers.

Family Child Care Contracts and Policies — Samples contracts and policies, and how - to information on using them effectively to improve tour business.

Family Day Caring magazine — The best source of information on every aspect of home-based child care.

Family Day Care Tax Workbook — Updated every year, latest step-by-step information on forms, depreciation, etc.

Heart to Heart Caregiving: A Sourcebook of Family Day Care Activities, Projects and Practical Provider Support — Excellent ideas and guidance written by an experienced provider.

Kids Encyclopedia of Things to Make and Do — Nearly 2,000 art and craft projects for children aged 4-10.

Open the Door, Let's Explore — Full of fun, inexpensive neighborhood walks and field trips designed to help young children.

S.O.S. Kit for Directors — Offers range of brainstormed solutions to everyday questions and problems.

Sharing in the Caring — Packet to help establish good relationships between providers and parents with agreement forms and other information.

Staff Orientation in Early Childhood Programs — Complete manual for orienting new staff on all program areas.

Survival Kit for Early Childhood Directors — Solutions, implementation steps and results to handling difficulties with children, staff, parents.

Teachables II — Similar to *Teachables From Trashables*; with another 75-plus toys.

Those Mean Nasty Dirty Downright Disgusting but... Invisible Germs — A delightful story that reinforces for children the benefits of frequent hand washing.